'Tuesday Lobsang Rampa, I know all about you, all that has been predicted. Your trial of endurance has been harsh but with good reason. That reason you will know in later years. Know now that of every thousand monks, only one is fitted for higher things, for higher development. You will be specially trained, intensively trained, and in a few short years you will be given more knowledge than a lama normally acquires in a long lifetime. The way will be hard, and often it will be painful. To force clairvoyance is painful, and to travel in the astral planes requires nerves that nothing can shatter, and a determination as hard as rocks. You will be given every assistance. Your Path is mapped for you, Tuesday Lobsang Rampa.'

THE THIRD EYE

T. Lobsang Rampa

The Third Eye

Illustrated by
TESSA THEOBALD

CORGI BOOKS
A DIVISION OF TRANSWORLD PUBLISHERS LTD

THE THIRD EYE
A CORGI BOOK 552 09834 5

Originally published in Great Britain
by Martin Secker & Warburg Ltd.

PRINTING HISTORY
Secker & Warburg edition published 1956
Secker & Warburg 9th impression 1958
Corgi edition published 1959
Corgi edition reprinted 1962
Corgi edition reprinted 1963
Corgi edition reprinted 1963
Corgi edition reissued 1965
Corgi edition reprinted 1966
Corgi edition reprinted 1967
Corgi edition reprinted 1968
Corgi edition reprinted 1969
Corgi edition reprinted 1970
Corgi edition reprinted 1971
Corgi edition reprinted 1971
Corgi edition reprinted 1972
Corgi edition reprinted 1973
Corgi edition reprinted 1973
Corgi edition reprinted 1974
Corgi edition reissued 1975

This book is set in 9/10 pt. Times.

Corgi Books are published by Transworld Publishers Ltd.,
Cavendish House, 57–59 Uxbridge Road,
Ealing, London, W.5.
Made and printed in Great Britain by
Hunt Barnard Printing Ltd., Aylesbury, Bucks.

To
E. E. G.,
a friend when few are,
in time of need.

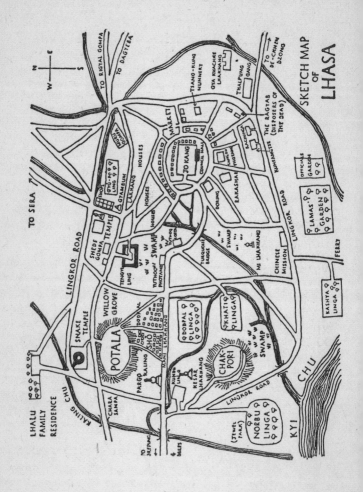

SKETCH MAP OF LHASA

CONTENTS

AUTHOR'S PREFACE

I AM a Tibetan. One of the few who have reached this strange Western world. The construction and grammar of this book leave much to be desired, but I have never had a formal lesson in the English language. My "School of English" was a Japanese prison camp, where I learned the language as best I could from English and American women prisoner patients. Writing in English was learned by "trial and error".

Now my beloved country is invaded—as predicted—by Communist hordes. For this reason only I have disguised my true name and that of my friends. Having done so much against Communism, I know that my friends in Communist countries will suffer if my identity can be traced. As I have been in Communist, as well as Japanese hands, I know from personal experience what torture can do, but it is not about torture that this book is written, but about a peace-loving country which has been so misunderstood and greatly misrepresented for so long.

Some of my statements, so I am told, may not be believed. That is your privilege, but Tibet is a country unknown to the rest of the world. The man who wrote, of another country, that "the people rode on turtles in the sea" was laughed to scorn. So were those who had seen "living-fossil" fish. Yet the latter have recently been discovered and a specimen taken in a refrigerated aeroplane to the U.S.A. for study. These men were disbelieved. They were eventually proved to be truthful and accurate. So will I be.

T. LOBSANG RAMPA

Written in the Year of the Wood Sheep.

CHAPTER ONE

EARLY DAYS AT HOME

"Oé. Oé. Four years old and can't stay on a horse! You'll never make a man! What will your noble father say?" With this, Old Tzu gave the pony—and luckless rider—a hearty thwack across the hindquarters, and spat in the dust.

The golden roofs and domes of the Potala gleamed in the brilliant sunshine. Closer, the blue waters of the Serpent Temple lake rippled to mark the passing of the water-fowl. From farther along the stony track came the shouts and cries of men urging on the slow-moving yaks just setting out from Lhasa. From near by came the chest-shaking "bmmn, bmmn, bmmn" of the deep bass trumpets as monk musicians practised in the fields away from the crowds.

But I had no time for such everyday, commonplace things. Mine was the serious task of staying on my very reluctant pony. Nakkim had other things in mind. He wanted to be free of his rider, free to graze, and roll and kick his feet in the air.

Old Tzu was a grim and forbidding taskmaster. All his life he had been stern and hard, and now as guardian and riding instructor to a small boy of four, his patience often gave way under the strain. One of the men of Kham, he, with others, had been picked for his size and strength. Nearly seven feet tall he was, and broad with it. Heavily padded shoulders increased his apparent breadth. In eastern Tibet there is a district where the men are unusually tall and strong. Many were over seven feet tall, and these men were picked to act as police monks in all the lamaseries. They padded

11

their shoulders to increase their apparent size, blackened their faces to look more fierce, and carried long staves which they were prompt to use on any luckless malefactor.

Tzu had been a police monk, but now he was dry-nurse to a princeling! He was too badly crippled to do much walking, and so all his journeys were made on horseback. In 1904 the British, under Colonel Younghusband, invaded Tibet and caused much damage. Apparently they thought the easiest method of ensuring our friendship was to shell our buildings and kill our people. Tzu had been one of the defenders, and in the action he had part of his left hip blown away.

My father was one of the leading men in the Tibetan Government. His family, and that of mother, came within the upper ten families, and so between them my parents had considerable influence in the affairs of the country. Later I will give more details of our form of government.

Father was a large man, bulky, and nearly six feet tall. His strength was something to boast about. In his youth he could lift a pony off the ground, and he was one of the few who could wrestle with the men of Kham and come off best.

Most Tibetans have black hair and dark brown eyes. Father was one of the exceptions, his hair was chestnut brown, and his eyes were grey. Often he would give way to sudden bursts of anger for no reason that we could see.

We did not see a great deal of father. Tibet had been having troublesome times. The British had invaded us in 1904, and the Dalai Lama had fled to Mongolia, leaving my father and others of the Cabinet to rule in his absence. In 1909 the Dalai Lama returned to Lhasa after having been to Peking. In 1910 the Chinese, encouraged by the success of the British invasion, stormed Lhasa. The Dalai Lama again retreated, this time to India. The Chinese were driven from Lhasa in 1911 during the time of the Chinese Revolution, but not before they had committed fearful crimes against our people.

In 1912 the Dalai Lama again returned to Lhasa. During the whole time he was absent, in those most difficult days, father and the others of the Cabinet, had the full responsibility of ruling Tibet. Mother used to say that father's temper was never the same after. Certainly he had no time for us children, and we at no time had fatherly affection from him. I, in particular, seemed to arouse his ire, and I was left to the scant mercies of Tzu "to make or break", as father said.

My poor performance on a pony was taken as a personal insult by Tzu. In Tibet small boys of the upper class are taught to ride almost before they can walk. Skill on a horse is essential in a country where there is no wheeled traffic, where all journeys have to be done on foot or on horseback. Tibetan nobles practise horsemanship hour after hour, day after day. They can stand on the narrow wooden saddle of a galloping horse, and shoot first with a rifle at a moving target, then change to bow and arrow. Sometimes skilled riders will gallop across the plains in formation, and change horses by jumping from saddle to saddle. I, at four years of age, found it difficult to stay in one saddle!

My pony, Nakkim, was shaggy, and had a long tail. His narrow head was intelligent. He knew an astonishing number of ways in which to unseat an unsure rider. A favourite trick of his was to have a short run forward, then stop dead and lower his head. As I slid helplessly forward over his neck and on to his head he would raise it with a jerk so that I turned a complete somersault before hitting the ground. Then he would stand and look at me with smug complacency.

Tibetans never ride at a trot; the ponies are small and riders look ridiculous on a trotting pony. Most times a gentle amble is fast enough, with the gallop kept for exercise.

Tibet was a theocratic country. We had no desire for the "progress" of the outside world. We wanted only to be able to meditate and to overcome the limitations of the flesh. Our Wise Men had long realized that the West had coveted the riches of Tibet, and knew that when the foreigners came in, peace went out. Now the arrival of the Communists in Tibet has proved that to be correct.

My home was in Lhasa, in the fashionable district of Lingkhor, at the side of the ring road which goes all round Lhasa, and in the shadow of the Peak. There are three circles of roads, and the outer road, Lingkhor, is much used by pilgrims. Like all houses in Lhasa, at the time I was born ours was two stories high at the side facing the road. No one must look down on the Dalai Lama, so the limit is two stories. As the height ban really applies only to one procession a year, many houses have an easily dismantled wooden structure on their flat roofs for eleven months or so.

Our house was of stone and had been built for many years. It was in the form of a hollow square, with a large internal courtyard. Our animals used to live on the ground floor, and we lived upstairs. We were fortunate in having a flight of stone steps leading from the ground; most Tibetan houses have a ladder or, in the peasants' cottages, a notched pole which one uses at dire risk to one's shins. These notched poles became very slippery indeed with use, hands covered with yak butter transferred it to the pole and the peasant who forgot, made a rapid descent to the floor below.

In 1910, during the Chinese invasion, our house had been partly wrecked and the inner wall of the building was demolished. Father had it rebuilt four stories high. It did not overlook the Ring, and we could not look over the head of the Dalai Lama when in procession, so there were no complaints.

The gate which gave entrance to our central courtyard was heavy and black with age. The Chinese invaders has not been able to force its solid wooden beams, so they had broken down a wall instead. Just above this entrance was the office of the steward. He could see all who entered or left. He engaged—and dismissed—staff and saw that the household was run efficiently. Here, at his window, as the sunset trumpets blared from the monasteries, came the beggars of Lhasa to receive a meal to sustain them through the darkness of the night. All the leading nobles made provision for the poor of their district. Often chained convicts would come, for there are few prisons in Tibet, and the convicted wandered the streets and begged for their food.

In Tibet convicts are not scorned or looked upon as pariahs. We realized that most of us would be convicts—if we were found out—so those who were unfortunate were treated reasonably.

Two monks lived in rooms to the right of the steward; these were the household priests who prayed daily for divine approval of our activities. The lesser nobles had one priest, but our position demanded two. Before any event of note, these priests were consulted and asked to offer prayers for the favour of the gods. Every three years the priests returned to the lamaseries and were replaced by others.

In each wing of our house there was a chapel. Always the butter-lamps were kept burning before the carved wooden altar. The seven bowls of holy water were cleaned and replenished several times a day. They had to be clean, as the gods might want to come and drink from them. The priests were well fed, eating the same food as the family, so that they could pray better and tell the gods that our food was good.

To the left of the steward lived the legal expert, whose job it was to see that the household was conducted in a proper and legal manner. Tibetans are very law-abiding, and father had to be an outstanding example in observing the law.

We children, brother Paljör, sister Yasodhara, and I, lived in the new block, at the side of the square remote from the road. To our left we had a chapel, to the right was the schoolroom which the children of the servants also attended. Our lessons were long and varied. Paljör did not inhabit the body long. He was weakly and unfit for the hard life to which we both were subjected. Before he was seven he left us and returned to the Land of Many Temples. Yaso was six when he passed over, and I was four. I still remember how they came for him as he lay, an empty husk, and how the Men of the Death carried him away to be broken up and fed to the scavenger birds according to custom.

Now Heir to the Family, my training was intensified. I was four years of age and a very indifferent horseman. Father was indeed a strict man and as a Prince of the Church he saw to it that his son had stern discipline, and was an example of how others should be brought up.

In my country, the higher the rank of a boy, the more severe his training. Some of the nobles were beginning to think that boys should have an easier time, but not father. His attitude was: a poor boy had no hope of comfort later, so give him kindness and consideration while he was young. The higher-class boy had all riches and comforts to expect in later years, so be quite brutal with him during boyhood and youth, so that he should experience hardship and show consideration for others. This also was the official attitude of the country. Under this system weaklings did not survive, but those who did could survive almost anything.

Tzu occupied a room on the ground floor and very near the main gate. For years he had, as a police monk, been able to see all manner of people and now he could not bear to be in seclusion, away from it all. He lived near the stables in which father kept his twenty horses and all the ponies and work animals.

The grooms hated the sight of Tzu, because he was officious and interfered with their work. When father went riding he had to have six armed men escort him. These men wore uniform, and Tzu always bustled about them, making sure that everything about their equipment was in order.

For some reason these six men used to back their horses against a wall, then, as soon as my father appeared on his horse, they would charge forward to meet him. I found that if I leaned out of a storeroom window, I could touch one of the riders as he sat on his horse. One day, being idle, I cautiously passed a rope through his stout leather belt as he was fiddling with his equipment. The two ends I looped and passed over a hook inside the window. In the bustle and talk I was not noticed. My father appeared, and the riders surged forward. Five of them. The sixth was pulled backwards off his horse, yelling that demons were gripping him. His belt broke, and in the confusion I was able to pull away the rope and steal away undetected. It gave me much pleasure, later, to say: "So you too, Ne-tuk, can't stay on a horse!"

Our days were quite hard, we were awake for eighteen hours out of the twenty-four. Tibetans believe that it is not wise to sleep at all when it is light, or the demons of the day may come and seize one. Even very small babies are kept awake so that they shall not become demon-infested. Those who are ill also have to be kept awake, and a monk is called in for this. No one is spared from it, even people who are dying have to be kept conscious for as long as possible, so that they shall know the right road to take through the border lands to the next world.

At school we had to study languages, Tibetan and Chinese. Tibetan is two distinct languages, the ordinary and the honorific. We used the ordinary when speaking to servants and those of lesser rank, and the honorific to those of equal or superior rank. The horse of a higher-rank person had to be addressed in honorific style! Our autocratic cat, stalking across the courtyard on some mysterious business, would be addressed by a servant: "Would honourable Puss Puss deign to come and drink this unworthy milk?" No matter how "honourable Puss Puss" was addressed, she would never come until she was ready.

Our schoolroom was quite large, at one time it had been used as a refectory for visiting monks, but since the new buildings were finished, that particular room had been made into a school for the estate. Altogether there were about sixty children attending. We sat cross-legged on the floor, at a table, or long bench, which was about eighteen inches high. We sat with our backs to the teacher, so that we did not know when he was looking at us. It made us

16

work hard all the time. Paper in Tibet is hand-made and expensive, far too expensive to waste on children. We used slates, large thin slabs about twelve inches by fourteen inches. Our "pencils" were a form of hard chalk which could be picked up in the Tsu La Hills, some twelve thousand feet higher than Lhasa, which was already twelve thousand feet above sea-level. I used to try to get the chalks with a reddish tint, but sister Yaso was very very fond of a soft purple. We could obtain quite a number of colours: reds, yellows, blues, and greens. Some of the colours, I believe, were due to the presence of metallic ores in the soft chalk base. Whatever the cause, we were glad to have them.

Arithmetic really bothered me. If seven hundred and eighty-three monks each drank fifty-two cups of tsampa per day, and each cup held five-eighths of a pint, what size container would be needed for a week's supply? Sister Yaso could do these things and think nothing of it. I, well, I was not so bright.

I came into my own when we did carving. That was a subject which I liked and could do reasonably well. All printing in Tibet is done from carved wooden plates, and so carving was considered to be quite an asset. We children could not have wood to waste. The wood was expensive as it had to be brought all the way from India. Tibetan wood was too tough and had the wrong kind of grain. We used a soft kind of soapstone material, which could be cut easily with a sharp knife. Sometimes we used stale yak cheese!

One thing that was never forgotten was a recitation of the Laws. These we had to say as soon as we entered the schoolroom, and again just before we were allowed to leave. These Laws were:

> Return good for good.
> Do not fight with gentle people.
> Read the Scriptures and understand them.
> Help your neighbours.
> The Law is hard on the rich to teach them understanding and equity.
> The Law is gentle with the poor to show them compassion.
> Pay your debts promptly.

So that there was no possibility of forgetting, these Laws were carved on banners and fixed to the four walls of our schoolroom.

Life was not all study and gloom though; we played as hard as we studied. All our games were designed to toughen us and enable us to survive in hard Tibet with its extremes of temperature. At noon, in summer, the temperature may be as high as eighty-five degrees Fahrenheit, but that same summer's night it may drop to forty degrees below freezing. In winter it was often very much colder than this.

Archery was good fun and it did develop muscles. We used bows made of yew, imported from India, and sometimes we made crossbows from Tibetan wood. As Buddhists we never shot at living targets. Hidden servants would pull a long string and cause a target to bob up or down—we never knew which to expect. Most of the others could hit the target when standing on the saddle of a galloping pony. I could never stay on that long! Long jumps were a different matter. Then there was no horse to bother about. We ran as fast as we could, carrying a fifteen-foot pole, then when our speed was sufficient, jumped with the aid of the pole. I used to say that the others stuck on a horse so long that they had no strength in their legs, but I, who had to use my legs, really could vault. It was quite a good system for crossing streams, and very satisfying to see those who were trying to follow me plunge in one after the other.

Stilt walking was another of our pastimes. We used to dress up and become giants, and often we would have fights on stilts—the one who fell off was the loser. Our stilts were home-made, we could not just slip round to the nearest shop and buy such things. We used all our powers of persuasion on the Keeper of the Stores— usually the Steward—so that we could obtain suitable pieces of wood. The grain had to be just right, and there had to be freedom from knotholes. Then we had to obtain suitable wedge-shaped pieces of footrests. As wood was too scarce to waste, we had to wait our opportunity and ask at the most appropriate moment.

The girls and young women played a form of shuttlecock. A small piece of wood had holes made in one upper edge, and feathers were wedged in. The shuttlecock was kept in the air by using the feet. The girl would lift her skirt to a suitable height to permit of free kicking and from then on would use her feet only, to touch with the hand meant that she was disqualified. An active girl would keep the thing in the air for as long as ten minutes at a time before missing a kick.

The real interest in Tibet, or at least in the district of Ü which is the home county of Lhasa, was kite flying. This could be called a national sport. We could only indulge in it at certain times, at certain seasons. Years before it had been discovered that if kites were flown in the mountains, rain fell in torrents, and in those days it was thought that the Rain Gods were angry, so kite flying was permitted only in the autumn, which in Tibet is the dry season. At certain times of the year, men will not shout in the mountains, as the reverberation of their voices causes the super-saturated rain-clouds from India to shed their load too quickly and cause rainfall in the wrong place. Now, on the first day of autumn, a long kite would be sent up from the roof of the Potala. Within minutes, kites of all shapes, sizes, and hues made their appearance over Lhasa, bobbing and twisting in the strong breeze.

I loved kite flying and I saw to it that my kite was one of the first to soar upwards. We all made our own kites, usually with a bamboo framework, and almost always covered with fine silk. We had no difficulty in obtaining this good quality material, it was a point of honour for the household that the kite should be of the finest class. Of box form, we frequently fitted them with a ferocious dragon head and with wings and tail.

We had battles in which we tried to bring down the kites of our rivals. We stuck shards of broken glass to the kite string, and covered part of the cord with glue powdered with broken glass in the hope of being able to cut the strings of others and so capture the falling kite.

Sometimes we used to steal out at night and send out kites aloft with little butter-lamps inside the head and body. Perhaps the eyes would glow red, and the body would show different colours against the dark night sky. We particularly liked it when the huge yak caravans were expected from the Lho-dzong district. In our childish innocence we thought that the ignorant natives from far distant places would not know about such "modern" inventions as our kites, so we used to set out to frighten some wits into them.

One device of ours was to put three different shells into the kites in a certain way, so that when the wind blew into them, they would produce a weird wailing sound. We likened it to fire-breathing dragons shrieking in the night, and we hoped that its effect on the traders would be salutary. We had many a delicious tingle along our spines as we thought of these men lying frightened in their bed-rolls as our kites bobbed above.

Although I did not know it at this time, my play with kites was to stand me in very good stead in later life when I actually flew in them. Now it was but a game, although an exciting one. We had one game which could have been quite dangerous: we made large kites—big things about seven or eight feet square and with wings projecting from two sides. We used to lay these on level ground near a ravine where there was a particularly strong updraught of air. We would mount our ponies with one end of the cord looped round our waists, and then we would gallop off as fast as our ponies would move. Up into the air jumped the kite and soaring higher and higher until it met this particular updraught. There would be a jerk and the rider would be lifted straight off his pony, perhaps ten feet in the air and sink swaying slowly to earth. Some poor wretches were almost torn in two if they forgot to take their feet from the stirrups, but I, never very good on a horse, could always fall off, and to be lifted was a pleasure. I found, being foolishly adventurous, that if I yanked at a cord at the moment of rising I would go higher, and further judicious yanks would enable me to prolong my flights by seconds.

On one occasion I yanked most enthusiastically, the wind co-operated, and I was carried on to the flat roof of a peasant's house upon which was stored the winter fuel.

Tibetan peasants live in houses with flat roofs with a small parapet, which retains the yak dung, which is dried and used as fuel. This particular house was of dried mud brick instead of the more usual stone, nor was there a chimney: an aperture in the roof served to discharge smoke from the fire below. My sudden arrival at the end of a rope disturbed the fuel and as I was dragged across the roof, I scooped most of it through the hole on to the unfortun-ate inhabitants below.

I was not popular. My appearance, also through that hole, was greeted with yelps of rage and, after having one dusting from the furious householder, I was dragged off to father for another dose of corrective medicine. That night I lay on my face!

The next day I had the unsavoury job of going through the stables and collecting yak dung, which I had to take to the peasant's house and replace on the roof, which was quite hard work, as I was not yet six years of age. But everyone was satisfied except me; the other boys had a good laugh, the peasant now had twice as much fuel, and father had demonstrated that he was a strict and just man. And I? I spent the next night on my face as well, and I was not sore with horseriding!

It may be thought that all this was very hard treatment, but Tibet has no place for weaklings. Lhasa is twelve thousand feet above sea-level, and with extremes of temperature. Other districts are higher, and the conditions even more arduous, and weaklings could very easily imperil others. For this reason, and not because of cruel intent, training was strict.

At the higher altitudes people dip new-born babies in icy streams to test if they are strong enough to be allowed to live. Quite often I have seen little processions approaching such a stream, perhaps seventeen thousand feet above the sea. At its banks the procession will stop, and the grandmother will take the baby. Around her will be grouped the family: father, mother, and close relatives. The baby will be undressed, and grandmother will stoop and immerse the little body in the water, so that only the head and mouth are exposed to the air. In the bitter cold the baby turns red, then blue, and its cries of protest stop. It looks dead, but grandmother has much experience of such things, and the little one is lifted from the water, dried, and dressed. If the baby survives, then it is as the gods decree. If it dies, then it has been spared much suffering on earth. This really is the kindest way in such a frigid country. Far better that a few babies die then that they should be incurable invalids in a country where there is scant medical attention.

With the death of my brother it became necessary to have my studies intensified, because when I was seven years of age I should have to enter upon training for whatever career the astrologers suggested. In Tibet everything is decided by astrology, from the buying of a yak to the decision about one's career. Now the time was approaching, just before my seventh birthday, when mother would give a really big party to which nobles and others of high rank would be invited to hear the forecast of the astrologers.

Mother was decidedly plump, she had a round face and black hair. Tibetan women wear a sort of wooden framework on their head, and over this the hair is draped to make it as ornamental as possible. These frames were very elaborate affairs, they were frequently of crimson lacquer, studded with semi-precious stones and inlaid with jade and coral. With well-oiled hair the effect was very brilliant.

Tibetan women use very gay clothes, with many reds and greens and yellows. In most instances there would be an apron of one colour, with a vivid horizontal stripe of a contrasting but harmonious colour. Then there was the earring at the left ear, its size depending on the rank of the wearer. Mother, being a member of one of the leading families, had an earring more than six inches long.

We believed that women should have absolutely equal rights with men, but in the running of the house mother went further than that and was the undisputed dictator, an autocrat who knew what she wanted and always got it.

In the stir and flurry of preparing the house and the grounds for the party, she was indeed in her element. There was organizing to be done, commands to be given, and new schemes to outshine the neighbours to be thought out. She excelled at this; having travelled extensively with father to India, Peking, and Shanghai, she had a wealth of foreign thought at her disposal.

The date having been decided for the party, invitations were carefully written out by monk-scribes on the thick, hand-made paper which was always used for communications of the highest importance. Each invitation was about twelve inches wide by about two feet long: each invitation bore father's family seal, and, as mother was also of the upper ten, her seal had to go on as well. Father and mother had a joint seal, this bringing the total to three. Altogether the invitations were most imposing documents. It frightened me immensely to think that all this fuss was solely about me. I did not know that I was really of secondary importance, and that the Social Event came first. If I had been told that the magnificence of the party would confer great prestige upon my parents, it would have conveyed absolutely nothing to me, so I went on being frightened.

We had engaged special messengers to deliver these invitations; each man was mounted on a thoroughbred horse. Each carried a cleft stick, in which was lodged an invitation. The stick was surmounted by a replica of the family coat of arms. The sticks were

gaily decorated with printed prayers which waved in the wind. There was pandemonium in the courtyard as all the messengers got ready to leave at the same time. The attendants were hoarse with shouting, horses were neighing, and the huge black mastiffs were barking madly. There was a last-minute gulping of Tibetan beer before the mugs were put down with a clatter as the ponderous main gates rumbled open, and the troop of men with wild yells galloped out.

In Tibet messengers deliver a written message, but also give an oral version which may be quite different. In days of long ago, bandits would waylay messengers and act upon the written message, perhaps attacking an ill-defended house or procession. It became the habit to write a misleading message which often lured bandits to where they could be captured. This old custom of written and oral messages was a survival of the past. Even now, sometimes the two messages would differ, but the oral version was always accepted as correct.

Inside the house everything was bustle and turmoil. The walls were cleaned and recoloured, the floors were scraped and the wooden boards polished until they were really dangerous to walk upon. The carved wooden altars in the main rooms were polished and relacquered and many new butter lamps were put in use. Some of these lamps were gold and some were silver, but they were all polished so much that it was difficult to see which was which. All the time mother and the head steward were hurrying around, criticizing here, ordering there, and generally giving the servants a miserable time. We had more than fifty servants at the time, and others were engaged for the forthcoming occasion. They were all kept busy, but they all worked with a will. Even the courtyard was scraped until the stones shone as if newly quarried. The spaces between them were filled with coloured material to add to the gap appearance. When all this was done, the unfortunate servants were called before mother and commanded to wear only the cleanest of clean clothes.

In the kitchens there was tremendous activity; food was being prepared in enormous quantities. Tibet is a natural refrigerator, food can be prepared and kept for an almost indefinite time. The climate is very, very cold, and dry with it. But even when the temperature rises, the dryness keeps stored food good. Meat will keep for about a year, while grain keeps for hundreds of years.

Buddhists do not kill, so the only meat available is from animals which have fallen over cliffs, or been killed by accident. Our larders were well stocked with such meat. There are butchers in Tibet, but they are of an "untouchable" caste, and the more orthodox families do not deal with them at all.

Mother had decided to give the guests a rare and expensive treat. She was going to give them preserved rhododendron blooms. Weeks before, servants had ridden out from the courtyard to go to the foothills of the Himalaya where the choicest blooms were to be found. In our country, rhododendron trees grow to a huge size, and with an astonishing variety of colours and scents. Those blooms which have not quite reached maturity are picked and most carefully washed. Carefully, because if there is any bruising, the preserve will be ruined. Then each flower is immersed in a mixture of water and honey in a large glass jar, with special care to avoid trapping any air. The jar is sealed, and every day for weeks after the jars are placed in the sunlight and turned at regular intervals, so that all parts of the flower are adequately exposed to the light. The flower grows slowly, and becomes filled with nectar manufactured from the honey-water. Some people like to expose the flower to the air for a few days before eating, so that it dries and

23

becomes a little crisp, but without losing flavour or appearance. These people also sprinkle a little sugar on the petals to imitate snow. Father grumbled about the expense of these preserves: "We could have bought ten yak with calves for what you have spent on these pretty flowers," he said. Mother's reply was typical of women: "Don't be a fool! We must make a show, and anyhow, this is *my* side of the house."

Another delicacy was shark's fin. This was brought from China sliced up, and made into soup. Someone had said that "shark's fin soup is the world's greatest gastronomic treat". To me the stuff tasted terrible; it was an ordeal to swallow it, especially as by the time it reached Tibet, the original shark owner would not have recognized it. To state it mildly, it was slightly "off". That, to some, seemed to enhance the flavour.

My favourite was succulent young bamboo shoots, also brought from China. These could be cooked in various ways, but I preferred them raw with just a dab of salt. My choice was just the newly opening yellow-green ends. I am afraid that many shoots, before cooking, lost their ends in a manner at which the cook could only guess and not prove! Rather a pity, because the cook also preferred them that way.

Cooks in Tibet are men; women are no good at stirring tsampa, or making exact mixtures. Women take a handful of this, slap in a lump of that, and season with hope that it will be right. Men are more thorough, more painstaking, and so better cooks. Women are all right for dusting, talking, and, of course, for a few other things. Not for making tsampa, though.

Tsampa is the main food of Tibetans. Some people live on tsampa and tea from their first meal in life to their last. It is made from barley which is roasted to a nice crisp golden brown. Then the barley kernels are cracked so that the flour is exposed, then it is roasted again. This flour is then put in a bowl, and hot buttered tea is added. The mixture is stirred until it attains the consistency of dough. Salt, borax, and yak butter are added to taste. The result —tsampa—can be rolled into slabs, made into buns, or even moulded into decorative shapes. Tsampa is monotonous stuff alone, but it really is a very compact, concentrated food which will sustain life at all altitudes and under all conditions.

While some servants were making tsampa, others were making butter. Our butter-making methods could not be commended on hygienic grounds. Our churns were large goat-skin bags, with the hair inside. They were filled with yak or goat milk and the neck was then twisted, turned over, and tied to make it leakproof. The whole thing was then bumped up and down until butter was formed. We had a special butter-making floor which had stone protuberances about eighteen inches high. The bags full of milk were lifted and dropped on to these protuberances, which had the effect of "churning" the milk. It was monotonous to see and hear perhaps ten servants lifting and dropping these bags hour after hour. There was the indrawn "uh uh" as the bag was lifted, and the squashy "zunk" as it was dropped. Sometimes a carelessly handled or old bag would burst. I remember one really hefty fellow who was showing off his strength. He was working twice as fast as anyone else, and the veins were standing out on his neck with the exertion. Someone said: "You are getting old, Timon, you are slowing up." Timon grunted with rage and grasped the neck of the bag in his mighty hands; lifted it, and dropped the bag down. But his strength had done its work. The bag dropped, but Timon still had his hands—and the neck—in the air. Square on the stone protuberance dropped the bag. Up shot a column of half-formed butter. Straight into the face of a stupefied Timon it went. Into his mouth, eyes, ears, and hair. Running down his body, covering him with twelve to fifteen gallons of golden slush.

Mother, attracted by the noise, rushed in. It was the only time I have known her to be speechless. It may have been rage at the loss of the butter, or because she thought the poor fellow was choking, but she ripped off the torn goat-skin and thwacked poor Timon over the head with it. He lost his footing on the slippery floor, and dropped into the spreading butter mess.

Clumsy workers, such as Timon, could ruin the butter. If they were careless when plunging the bags on to the protruding stones, they would cause the hair inside the bags to tear loose and become mixed with the butter. No one minded picking a dozen or two hairs out of the butter, but whole wads of it was frowned upon. Such butter was set aside for use in the lamps or for distribution to beggars, who would heat it and strain it through a piece of cloth. Also set aside for beggars were the "mistakes" in culinary preparations. If a household wanted to let the neighbours know what a high standard was set, really good food was prepared and set before the beggars as "mistakes". These happy, well-fed gentlemen would then wander round to the other houses saying how well they had eaten. The neighbours would respond by seeing that the beggars had a very good meal. There is much to be said for the life of a beggar in Tibet. They never want; by using the "tricks of their trade" they can live exceedingly well. There is no disgrace in begging in most of the Eastern countries. Many monks beg their way from lamasery to lamasery. It is a recognized practice and is not considered any worse than is, say, collecting for charities in other countries. Those who feed a monk on his way are considered to have done a good deed. Beggars, too, have their code. If a man gives to a beggar, that beggar will stay out of the way and will not approach the donor again for a certain time.

The two priests attached to our household also had their part in the preparations for the coming event. They went to each animal carcase in our larders and said prayers for the souls of the animals who had inhabited those bodies. It was our belief that if an animal was killed—even by accident—and eaten, humans would be under a debt to that animal. Such debts were paid by having a priest pray over the animal body in the hope of ensuring that the animal reincarnated into a higher status in the next life upon earth. In the lamaseries and temples some monks devoted their whole time praying for animals. Our priests had the task of praying over the horses, before a long journey, prayers to avoid the horses becoming too tired. In this connection, our horses were never worked for two days together. If a horse was ridden on one day, then it had to be rested the next day. The same rule applied to the work animals. And they all knew it. If, by any chance a horse was picked for riding, and it had been ridden the day before, it would just stand still and refuse to move. When the saddle was removed, it would turn away with a shake of the head as if to say: "Well, I'm glad *that* injustice has been removed!" Donkeys were worse. They would wait until they were loaded, and then they would lie down and try to roll on the load.

We had three cats, and they were on duty all the time. One lived in the stables and exercised a stern discipline over the mice. They had to be very wary mice to remain mice and not cat-food. Another cat lived in the kitchen. He was elderly, and a bit of a simpleton. His mother had been frightened by the guns of the Younghusband Expedition in 1904, and he had been born too soon and was the only one of the litter to live. Appropriately, he was called "Younghusband". The third cat was a very respectable matron who lived with us. She was a model of maternal duty, and did her utmost to see that the cat population was not allowed to fall. When not engaged as nurse to her kittens, she used to follow mother about from room to room. She was small and black, and in spite of having a hearty appetite, she looked like a walking skeleton. Tibetan animals are not pets, nor are they slaves, they are beings with a useful purpose to serve, being with rights just as human beings have rights. According to Buddhist belief, all animals, all creatures in fact, have souls, and are reborn to earth in successively higher stages.

Quickly the replies to our invitations came in. Men came

galloping up to our gates brandishing the cleft messenger-sticks. Down from his room would come the steward to do honour to the messenger of the nobles. The man would snatch his message from the stick, and gasp out the verbal version. Then he would sag at the knees and sink to the ground with exquisite histrionic art to indicate that he had given all his strength to deliver his message to the House of Rampa. Our servants would play their part by crowding round with many clucks: "Poor fellow, he made a wonderfully quick journey. Burst his heart with the speed, no doubt. Poor, noble fellow!" I once disgraced myself completely by piping up: "Oh no he hasn't. I saw him resting a little way out so that he could make a final dash." It will be discreet to draw a veil of silence over the painful scene which followed.

At last the day arrived. The day I dreaded, when my career was to be decided for me, with no choice on my part. The first rays of the sun were peeping over the distant mountains when a servant dashed into my room. "What? Not up yet, Tuesday Lobsang Rampa? My, you *are* a lie-a-bed! It's four o'clock, and there is much to be done. *Get up!*" I pushed aside my blanket and got to my feet. For me this day was to point the path of my life.

In Tibet, two names are given, the first being the day of the week on which one was born. I was born on a Tuesday, so Tuesday was my first name. Then Lobsang, that was the name given to me by my parents. But if a boy should enter a lamasery he would be given another name, his "monk name". Was I to be given another name? Only the passing hours would tell. I, at seven, wanted to be a boatman swaying and tossing on the River Tsang-po, forty miles away. But wait a minute; *did* I? Boatmen are of low caste because they use boats of yak hide stretched over wooden formers. Boatman? Low caste? *No!* I wanted to be a professional flyer of kites. That was better, to be as free as the air, much better than being in a degrading little skin boat drifting on a turgid stream. A kite flyer, that is what I would be, and make wonderful kites with huge heads and glaring eyes. But today the priest-astrologers would have their say. Perhaps I'd left it a bit late, I could not get out of the window and escape now. Father would soon send men to bring me back. No, after all, I was a Rampa, and had to follow the steps of tradition. Maybe the astrologers would say that I should be a kite flyer. I could only wait and see.

CHAPTER TWO

END OF MY CHILDHOOD

"Ow! Yulgye, you are pulling my head off! I shall be as bald as a monk if you don't stop."

"Hold your peace, Tuesday Lobsang. Your pigtail must be straight and well buttered or your Honourable Mother will be after my skin."

"But Yulgye, you don't have to be so rough, you are twisting my head off."

"Oh, I can't bother about that, I'm in a hurry."

So there I was, sitting on the floor, with a tough man-servant winding me up by the pigtail! Eventually the wretched thing was as stiff as a frozen yak, and shining like moonlight on a lake.

Mother was in a whirl, moving round so fast that I felt almost as if I had several mothers. There were last-minute orders, final preparations, and much excited talk. Yaso, two years older than I, was bustling about like a woman of forty. Father had shut himself in his private room and was well out of the uproar. I wished I could have joined him!

For some reason mother had arranged for us to go to the Jo-kang, the Cathedral of Lhasa. Apparently we had to give a religious atmosphere to the later proceedings. At about ten in the morn.ng (Tibetan times are very elastic), a triple-toned gong was sounded to call us to our assembly point. We all mounted ponies: father, mother, Yaso, and about five others, including a very reluctant me. We turned across the Lingkhor road, and left at the foot of the Potala. This is a mountain of buildings, four hundred feet high and twelve hundred feet long. Past the village of Shö we went, along the plain of the Kyi Chu, until half an hour later we stood in front of the Jo-kang. Around it clustered small houses, shops and stalls to lure the pilgrims. Thirteen hundred years the Cathedral had stood here to welcome the devout. Inside, the stone floors were grooved inches deep by the passage of so many worshippers. Pilgrims moved reverently around the Inner Circuit, each turning the hundreds of prayer-wheels as they passed, and repeating incessantly the mantra: Om! Mani padme Hum!

Huge wooden beams, black with age, supported the roof, and the heavy odour of constantly burning incense drifted around like light summer clouds at the crest of a mountain. Around the walls were golden statues of the deities of our faith. Stout metal screens, with a coarse mesh so as not to obstruct the view, protected the statues from those whose cupidity overcame their reverence. Most of the more familiar statues were partly buried by the precious stones and gems which had been heaped around them by the pious who had sought favours. Candlesticks of solid gold held candles which burned continually, and whose light had not been extinguished during the past thirteen hundred years. From dark recesses came the sounds of bells, gongs, and the lowing bray of the conches. We made our circuit as tradition demanded.

Our devotions completed, we went on to the flat roof. Only the favoured few could visit here; father, as one of the Custodians, always came.

Our form of governments (yes, plural), may be of interest.

At the head of the State and Church, the final Court of Appeal, there was the Dalai Lama. Anyone in the country could petition him. If the petition or request was fair, or if an injustice had been done, the Dalai Lama saw that the request was granted, or the injustice rectified. It is not unreasonable to say that everyone in the country, probably without exception, either loved or revered him. He was an autocrat; he used power and domination, but *never* did he use these for his own gain, only for the good of the country. He knew of the coming Communist invasion, even though it lay many years ahead, and temporary eclipse of freedom, that is why a very small number of us were specially trained so that the arts of the priests should not be forgotten.

After the Dalai Lama there were two Councils, that is why I wrote "governments". The first was the Ecclesiastical Council. The four members of it were monks of Lama status. They were responsible, under the Inmost One, for all the affairs of the lamaseries and nunneries. All ecclesiastical matters came before them.

The Council of Ministers came next. This Council had four members, three lay and one cleric. They dealt with the affairs of

29

the country as a whole, and were responsible for integrating the Church and State.

Two officials, who may be termed Prime Ministers, for that is what they were, acted as "Liaison Officers" between the two Councils, and put their views before the Dalai Lama. They were of considerable importance during the rare meetings of the National Assembly. This was a body of some fifty men representing all the most important families and lamaseries in Lhasa. They met only during the gravest emergencies, such as in 1904, when the Dalai Lama went to Mongolia when the British invaded Lhasa. In connection with this, many Western people have the strange notion that the Inmost One was cowardly in "running away". He did *not* "run away". Wars on Tibet may be likened to a game of chess. If the king is taken, the game is won. The Dalai Lama was our "king". Without him there would be nothing to fight for: he *had* to go to safety in order to keep the country together. Those who accuse him of cowardice in any form simply do not know what they are talking about.

The National Assembly could be increased to nearly four hundred members when all the leaders from the provinces came in. There are five provinces: The Capital, as Lhasa was often called, was in the province of U-Tsang. Shigatse is in the same district. Gartok is western Tibet, Chang is northern Tibet, while Kham and Lho-dzong are the eastern and southern provinces respectively. With the passage of the years the Dalai Lama increased his power and did more and more without assistance from the Councils or Assembly. And never was the country better governed.

The view from the temple roof was superb. To the east stretched the Plain of Lhasa, green and lush and dotted with trees. Water sparkled through the trees, the rivers of Lhasa tinkling along to join the Tsang Po forty miles away. To the north and south rose the great mountain ranges enclosing our valley and making us seem secluded from the rest of the world. Lamaseries abounded on the lower levels. Higher, the small hermitages perched precariously on precipitous slopes. Westwards loomed the twin mountains of the Potala and Chakpori, the latter was known as the Temple of Medicine. Between these mountains the Western Gate glinted in the cold morning light. The sky was a deep purple emphasized by the pure white of the snow on the distant mountain ranges. Light, wispy clouds drifted high overhead. Much nearer, in the city itself, we looked down on the Council Hall nestling against the northern wall of the Cathedral. The Treasury was quite near, and surrounding it all were the stalls of the traders and the market in which one could buy almost anything. Close by, slightly to the east, a nunnery jostled the precincts of the Disposers of the Dead.

In the Cathedral grounds there was the never-ceasing babble of visitors to this, one of the most sacred places of Buddhism. The chatter of pilgrims who had travelled far, and who now brought gifts in the hope of obtaining a holy blessing. Some there were who brought animals saved from the butchers, and purchased with scarce money. There is much virtue in saving life, of animal and of man, and much credit would accrue.

As we stood gazing at the old, but ever-new scenes, we heard the rise and fall of monks' voices in psalmody, the deep bass of the older men and the high treble of the acolytes. There came the rumble and boom of the drums and the golden voices of the trumpets. Skirlings, and muffled throbs, and a sensation as of being caught up in a hypnotic net of emotions.

Monks bustled around dealing with their various affairs. Some with yellow robes and some in purple. The more numerous were in russet red, these were the "ordinary" monks. Those of much gold were from the Potala, as were those in cherry vestments. Acolytes in white, and police monks in dark maroon bustled about. All, or nearly all, had one thing in common: no matter how new their robes, they almost all had patches which were replicas of the patches on Buddha's robes. Foreigners who have seen Tibetan monks, or have seen pictures of them, sometimes remark on the "patched appearance". The patches, then, are part of the dress. The monks of the twelve-hundred-year-old Ne-Sar lamasery do it properly and have their patches of a lighter shade!

Monks wear the red robes of the Order; there are many shades of red caused by the manner in which the woollen cloth is dyed. Maroon to brick red, it is still "red". Certain official monks employed solely at the Potala wear gold sleeveless jackets over their red robes. Gold is a sacred colour in Tibet—gold is untarnishable and so always pure—and it is the official colour of the Dalai Lama. Some monks, or high lamas in personal attendance on the Dalai Lama, are permitted to wear gold robes *over* their ordinary red ones.

As we looked over the roof of the Jo-kang we could see many such gold-jacketed figures, and rarely one of the Peak officials. We looked up at the prayer-flags fluttering, and at the brilliant domes of the Cathedral. The sky looked beautiful, purple, with little flecks of wispy clouds, as if an artist had lightly flicked the canvas of heaven with a white-loaded brush. Mother broke the spell: "Well, we are wasting time, I shudder to think what the servants are doing. We must hurry!" So off on our patient ponies, clattering along the Lingkhor road, each step bringing me nearer to what I termed "The Ordeal", but which mother regarded as *her* "Big Day".

Back at home, mother had a final check of all that had been done and then we had a meal to fortify us for the events to come. We well knew that at times such as these, the guests would be well filled and well satisfied, but the poor hosts would be empty. There would be no time for us to eat later.

With much clattering of instruments, the monk-musicians arrived and were shown into the gardens. They were laden with trumpets, clarinets, gongs, and drums. Their cymbals were hung round their necks. Into the gardens they went, with much chatter, and called for beer to get them into the right mood for good playing. For the next half-hour there were horrible honks, and strident bleats from the trumpets as the monks prepared their instruments.

Uproar broke out in the courtyard as the first of the guests were sighted, riding in an armed cavalcade of men with fluttering pennants. The entrance gates were flung open, and two columns of our servants lined each side to give welcome to the arrivals. The steward was on hand with his two assistants who carried an assortment of the silk scarves which are used in Tibet as a form of salutation. There are eight qualities of scarves, and the correct one must be presented or offence may be implied! The Dalai Lama gives, and receives, only the first grade. We call these scarves "khata", and the method of presentation is this: the donor, if of equal rank, stands well back with the arms fully extended. The recipient also stands well back with arms extended. The donor makes a short bow and places the scarf across the wrists of the recipient, who bows, takes the scarf from the wrists, turns it over in approval, and hands it to a servant. In the case of a donor giving a scarf to a person of much higher rank, he or she kneels with tongue extended (a Tibetan greeting similar to lifting the hat) and places the khata at the feet of the recipient. The recipient in such cases places his scarf across the neck of the donor. In Tibet, gifts must always be accompanied by the appropriate khata, as must letters of congratulation. The Government used yellow scarves in place of the normal white. The Dalai Lama, if he desired to show the very highest honour to a person, would place a khata about a person's neck and would tie a red silk thread with a triple knot into the khata. If at the same time he showed his hands palm up—one was indeed honoured. We Tibetans are of the firm belief that one's whole history is written on the palm of the hand, and the Dalai Lama, showing his hands thus, would prove the friendliest intentions towards one. In later years I had this honour twice.

Our steward stood at the entrance, with an assistant on each side. He would bow to new arrivals, accept their khata, and pass it on to the assistant on the left. At the same time the assistant on his right would hand him the correct grade of scarf with which to return the salutation. This he would take and place across the wrists, or over the neck (according to rank), of the guest. All these scarves were used and re-used.

The steward and his assistants were becoming busy. Guests were arriving in large numbers. From neighbouring estates, from Lhasa city, and from outlying districts, they all came clattering along the Lingkhor road, to turn into our private drive in the shadow of the Potala. Ladies who had ridden a long distance wore a leather face-mask to protect the skin and complexion from the grit-laden wind. Frequently a crude resemblance of the wearer's features would be painted on the mask. Arrived at her destination, the lady would doff her mask as well as her yak-hide cloak. I was always fascinated by the features painted on the masks, the uglier or older the woman, the more beautiful and younger would be her mask-features!

In the house there was great activity. More and more seat-cushions were brought from the storerooms. We do not use chairs in Tibet, but sit cross-legged on cushions which are about two and a half feet square and about nine inches thick. The same cushions are used for sleeping upon, but then several are put together. To us they are far more comfortable than chairs or high beds.

Arriving guests were given buttered tea and led to a large room which had been converted into a refectory. Here they were able to choose refreshments to sustain them until the real party started. About forty women of the leading families had arrived, together with their women attendants. Some of the ladies were being entertained by mother, while others wandered around the house, inspecting the furnishings, and guessing their value. The place seemed to be overrun with women of all shapes, sizes, and ages. They appeared from the most unusual places, and did not hesitate one moment to ask passing servants what this cost, or what that was worth. They behaved, in short, like women the world over. Sister Yaso was parading around in very new clothes, with her hair done in what she regarded as the latest style, but which to me seemed terrible; but I was always biased when it came to women. Certain it was that on this day they seemed to get in the way.

There was another set of women to complicate matters: the high-class woman in Tibet was expected to have huge stores of clothing, and ample jewels. These she had to display, and as this would have entailed much changing and dressing, special girls—"chung girls"—were employed to act as mannequins. They paraded around in mother's clothes, sat and drank innumerable cups of butter-tea, and then went and changed into different clothing and jewellery. They mixed with the guests and became, to all intents and purposes, mother's assistant hostesses. Throughout the day these women would change their attire perhaps five or six times.

The men were more interested in the entertainers in the gardens. A troupe of acrobats had been brought in to add a touch of fun. Three of them held up a pole about fifteen feet high, and another acrobat climbed up and stood on his head on the top. Then the others snatched away the pole, leaving him to fall, turn, and land cat-like on his feet. Some small boys were watching, and immediately rushed away to a secluded spot to emulate the performance. They found a pole about eight or ten feet high, held it up, and the most daring climbed up and tried to stand on his head. Down he came, with an awful "crump", straight on top of the others. However, their heads were thick, and apart from egg-sized bruises, no harm was done.

Mother appeared, leading the rest of the ladies to see the

entertainments, and listen to the music. The latter was not difficult; the musicians were now well warmed up with copious amounts of Tibetan beer.

For this occasion, mother was particularly well dressed. She was wearing a yak-wool skirt of deep russet-red, reaching almost to the ankles. Her high boots of Tibetan felt were of the purest white, with blood-red soles, and tastefully arranged red piping.

Her bolero-type jacket was of a reddish-yellow, somewhat like father's monk robe. In my later medical days, I should have described it as "iodine on bandage"! Beneath it she wore a blouse of purple silk. These colours all harmonized, and had been chosen to represent the different classes of monks' garments.

Across her right shoulder was a silk brocade sash which was caught at the left side of her waist by a massive gold circlet. From the shoulder to the waist-knot the sash was blood red, but from that point it shaded from pale lemon-yellow to deep saffron when it reached the skirt hem.

Around her neck she had a gold cord which supported the three amulet bags which she always wore. These had been given to her on her marriage to father. One was from her family, one from father's family, and one, an unusual honour, was from the Dalai Lama. She wore much jewellery, because Tibetan women wear jewellery and ornaments in accordance with their station in life. A husband is expected to buy ornaments and jewellery whenever he has a rise in status.

Mother had been busy for days past having her hair arranged in a hundred and eight plaits, each about as thick as a piece of whip-cord. A hundred and eight is a Tibetan sacred number, and ladies with sufficient hair to make this number of plaits were considered to be most fortunate. The hair, parted in the Madonna style, was supported on a wooden framework worn on top of the head like a hat. Of red lacquered wood, it was studded with diamonds, jade, and gold discs. The hair trailed over it like rambler roses on a trellis.

Mother had a string of coral shapes depending from her ear. The weight was so great that she had to use a red thread around the ear to support it, or risk having the lobe torn. The earring reached nearly to her waist; I watched in fascination to see how she could turn her head to the left!

People were walking about, admiring the gardens, or sitting in groups discussing social affairs. The ladies, in particular, were busy with their talk. "Yes, my dear, Lady Doring is having a new floor laid. Finely ground pebbles polished to a high gloss." "Have you heard that that young lama who was staying with Lady

Rakasha . . ." etc. But everyone was really waiting for the main item of the day. All this was a mere warming-up for the events to come, when the priest-astrologers would forecast my future and direct the path I should take through life. Upon them depended the career I should undertake.

As the day grew old and the lengthening shadows crawled more quickly across the ground, the activities of the guests became slower. They were satiated with refreshments, and in a receptive mood. As the piles of food grew less, tired servants brought more and that, too, went with the passage of time. The hired entertainers grew weary and one by one slipped away to the kitchens for a rest and more beer.

The musicians were still in fine fettle, blowing their trumpets, clashing the cymbals, and thwacking the drums with gay abandon. With all the noise and uproar, the birds had been scared from their usual roosting places in the trees. And not only the birds were scared. The cats had dived precipitately into some safe refuge with the arrival of the first noisy guests. Even the huge black mastiffs which guarded the place were silent, their deep baying stilled in sleep. They had been fed and fed until they could eat no more.

In the walled gardens, as the day grew yet darker, small boys flitted like gnomes between the cultivated trees, swinging lighted butter-lamps and smoke incense censers, and at times leaping into the lower branches for a carefree frolic.

Dotted about the grounds were golden incense braziers sending up their thick columns of fragrant smoke. Attending them were old women who also twirled clacking prayer-wheels, each revolution of which sent thousands of prayers heavenwards.

Father was in a state of perpetual fright! His walled gardens were famous throughout the country for their expensive imported plants and shrubs. Now, to his way of thinking, the place was like a badly run zoo. He wandered around wringing his hands and uttering little moans of anguish when some guest stopped and fingered a bud. In particular danger were the apricot and pear trees, and the little dwarf apple trees. The larger and taller trees, poplar, willow, juniper, birch, and cypress, were festooned with streams of prayer-flags which fluttered gently in the soft evening breeze.

Eventually the day died as the sun set behind the far-distant peaks of the Himalaya. From the lamaseries came the sound of trumpets signalling the passing of yet another day, and with it hundreds of butter-lamps were set alight. They depended from the branches of trees, they swung from the projecting eaves of the houses, and others floated on the placid waters of the ornamental lake. Here they grounded, like boats on a sandbar, on the water-lily leaves, there they drifted towards the floating swans seeking refuge near the island.

The sound of a deep-toned gong, and everyone turned to watch the approaching procession. In the gardens a large marquee had been erected, with one completely open side. Inside was a raised dais on which were four of our Tibetan seats. Now the procession approached the dais. Four servants carried upright poles, with large flares at the upper end. Then came four trumpeters with silver trumpets sounding a fanfare. Following them, mother and father reached the dais and stepped upon it. Then two old men, very old men, from the lamasery of the State Oracle. These two old men from Nechung were the most experienced astrologers in the country. Their predictions have been proved correct time after time. Last week they had been called to predict for the Dalai Lama. Now they were going to do the same for a seven-year-old boy. For days they had been busy at their charts and computations. Long had been their discussions about trines, ecliptics, sesqui-quadrates, and the opposing influence of this or that. I will discuss astrology in a later chapter.

Two lamas carried the astrologers' notes and charts. Two others stepped forward and helped the old seers to mount the steps of the dais. Side by side they stood, like two old ivory carvings. Their gorgeous robes of yellow Chinese brocade merely emphasized their age. Upon their heads they wore tall priests' hats, and their wrinkled necks seemed to wilt beneath the weight.

People gathered around and sat on the ground on cushions brought by the servants. All gossip stopped, as people strained their ears to catch the shrill, piping voice of the astrologer-in-chief. "Lha dre mi cho-nang-chig," he said (Gods, devils, and men all behave in the same way), so the probable future can be foretold. On he droned, for an hour and then stopped for a ten-minute rest. For yet another hour he went on outlining the future. "Ha-le! Ha-le!" (Extraordinary! Extraordinary!), exclaimed the entranced audience.

And so it was foretold. A boy of seven to enter a lamasery, after a hard feat of endurance, and there be trained as a priest-surgeon. To suffer great hardships, to leave the homeland, and go among strange people. To lose all and have to start again, and eventually to succeed.

Gradually the crowd dispersed. Those who had come from afar would stay the night at our house and depart in the morning. Others would travel with their retinues and with flares to light the way. With much clattering of hooves, and the hoarse shouts of men, they assembled in the courtyard. Once again the ponderous gate swung open, and the company streamed through. Growing fainter in the distance was the clop-clop of the horses, and the chatter of their riders, until from without there was the silence of the night.

CHAPTER THREE

LAST DAYS AT HOME

INSIDE the house there was still much activity. Tea was still being consumed in huge quantities, and food was disappearing as last-minute revellers fortified themselves against the coming night. All the rooms were occupied, and there was no room for me. Disconsolately I wandered around, idly kicking at stones and anything else in the way, but even that did not bring inspiration. No one took any notice of me, the guests were tired and happy, the servants were tired and irritable. "The horses have more feeling," I grumbled to myself, "I will go and sleep with them."

The stables were warm, and the fodder was soft, but for a time sleep would not come. Each time I dozed a horse would nudge me, or a sudden burst of sound from the house would rouse me. Gradually the noises were stilled. I raised myself to one elbow and looked out, the lights were one by one flickering to blackness. Soon there was only the cold blue moonlight reflecting vividly from the snow-capped mountains. The horses slept, some on their feet, and some on their sides. I too slept. The next morning I was awakened by a rough shake and a voice saying: "Come along, Tuesday Lobsang. I have got to get the horses ready and you are in the way." So I got up and made my way into the house in search of food. There was much activity. People were preparing to leave, and mother was flitting from group to group for a last-minute chat. Father was discussing improvements to the house and to the gardens. He was telling an old friend of his that he intended having glass imported from India so that our house would have glazed windows. In Tibet there was no glass, none was made in the country, and the cost of bringing it from India was very high indeed. Tibetan windows have frames upon which is stretched paper which is highly waxed and translucent, but not transparent. Outside the windows were heavy wooden shutters, not so much to keep burglars away as to prevent the ingress of grit carried by the strong winds. This grit (sometimes it was more like small pebbles) would tear through any unprotected windows. It would also deeply cut exposed hands and faces, and during the season of strong winds, such journeys were fraught with danger. The people of Lhasa used to keep a wary eye upon the Peak and when it suddenly became hidden in a black haze everyone used to dash for shelter before the whipping, blood-bringing wind caught them. But not only humans were on the alert: animals also were on the watch, and it was no unusual sight to see horses and dogs leading the humans in the rush for shelter. Cats were *never* caught in a storm, and yaks were quite immune.

With the departure of the last of the guests I was called before father who said: "Go to the shopping centre and buy your needs. Tzu knows what is required." I thought of the things I would need: a tsampa bowl made of wood, a cup, and a rosary. The cup would be in three parts: a stand, the cup, and its lid. This would be of silver. The rosary would be of wood, with its hundred and eight beads highly polished. A hundred and eight, the sacred number, also indicates the things which a monk has to remember.

We set off, Tzu on his horse, and I on my pony. As we left the courtyard we turned right, later turning right again as we left the Ring Road past the Potala to enter the shopping centre. I looked about me as if seeing the town for the first time. I was greatly afraid that I was seeing it for the last time! The shops were crowded with chaffering merchants who had just arrived in Lhasa. Some were bringing tea from China, and others had brought cloth from India. We made our way through the crowd to the shops we wished to visit; every so often Tzu would call out a greeting to some old friend of former years.

I had to get a robe of russet red. I was going to have it rather on the large size, not merely because I was growing, but for an equally practical reason. In Tibet men wear voluminous robes which are tied tightly at the waist. The upper portion is pulled up and forms a pouch which is the repository for all those items which the Tibetan male finds it necessary to carry. The average monk, for instance, will carry in this pouch his tsampa bowl, cup, a knife, various amulets, a rosary, a bag of roasted barley and, not infrequently, a supply of tsampa. But remember, a monk carries upon his person all his worldly possessions.

My pathetic little purchases were rigidly supervised by Tzu, who permitted only the barest essentials, and those of merely mediocre quality as befitted a "poor acolyte". They included sandals with yak-leather soles, a small leather bag for roasted barley, a wooden tsampa bowl, wooden cup—not the silver affair I had hoped for!—and a carving knife. This, together with a very plain rosary which I had to polish myself, were to be my only possessions. Father was a millionaire several times over, with huge estates all over the country, with jewels, and indeed much gold. But I, while I was training, while father lived, I was to be just a very poor monk.

I looked again at the street, at those two-storied buildings with the long, projecting eaves. I looked again at the shops with the sharks' fins and the saddle covers displayed on the booths outside their doors. I listened once more to the cheerful banter of the traders and their customers haggling good-naturedly over the prices to be paid. The street had never looked more attractive and I thought of the fortunate people who saw it every day and would continue to see it every day.

Stray dogs ambled around, sniffing here and there, exchanging growls, horses neighed softly to each other as they awaited the pleasure of their masters. Yaks groaned throatily as they meandered through the pedestrian throng. What mysteries lurked behind those paper-covered windows. What wonderful stores of goods, from all parts of the world, had passed through those sturdy wooden doors, and what tales those open shutters would tell if they could speak.

41

All this I gazed upon as upon an old friend. It did not occur to me that I would ever see these streets again, even though but rarely. I thought of the things I would have liked to have done, of the things I would have liked to buy. My reverie was shatteringly interrupted. A hand immense and menacing descended upon me, caught my ear and twisted it fiercely, while the voice of Tzu bellowed for all the world to hear: "Come on, Tuesday Lobsang, are you dead on your feet? I don't know what boys are coming to nowadays. Wasn't like this when I was a lad." Tzu did not seem to mind if I stayed behind without my ear, or retained it by following him. There was no choice but to "come on". All the way home Tzu rode ahead, mumbling and groaning about the "present generation, good-for-nothing lot, bone-idle lay-abouts living in a daze". At least there was one bright spot, as we turned into the Lingkhor road there was a quite bitter wind. Tzu's great bulk ahead of me gave me a sheltered path.

At home, mother had a look at the things which I had bought. To my regret she agreed that they were good enough. I had been cherishing the hope that she would overrule Tzu, and say that I could have better quality articles. So once again my hopes of having a silver cup were shattered and I had to make do with the wooden one turned on a hand-lathe in the bazaars of Lhasa.

I was not to be left alone for my last week. Mother dragged me round to the other big houses in Lhasa so that I could pay my respects, not that I was feeling respectful! Mother revelled in the journeyings, in the interchange of social conversation, and in the polite tittle-tattle which made up the everyday round. I was bored stiff; to me all this was a genuine ordeal as I was definitely not born with the attributes which make one suffer fools gladly. I wanted to be out in the open enjoying myself for the few days remaining. I wanted to be out flying my kites, jumping with my pole, and practising archery, instead of which I had to be dragged around like a prize yak, being shown off to frumpish old women who had nothing to do all day but to sit on silk cushions and call for a servant in order to gratify their slightest whim.

But it was not only mother who caused me so much heart-burning. Father had to visit the Drebung Lamasery and I was taken along to see the place. Drebung is the largest lamasery in the world, with its ten thousand monks, its high temples, little stone houses, and terraced buildings rising tier upon tier. This community was like a walled town, and like a good town, it was self-supporting. Drebung means "Rice Heap", and from a distance it *did* look like a heap of rice, with the towers and domes gleaming in the light. Just at this time I was not in a mood to appreciate architectural beauties: I was feeling distinctly glum at having to waste precious time like this.

Father was busy with the abbot and his assistants, and I, like a waif of the storm, wandered disconsolately around. It made me shiver with fright when I saw how some of the small novices were treated. The Rice Heap was really seven lamaseries in one; seven distinct orders, seven separate colleges formed its composition. It was so large that no one man was in charge. Fourteen abbots ruled here and stern disciplinarians they were. I was glad when this "pleasant jaunt across a sunlit plain"—to quote father—came to an end, but more glad to know that I was *not* going to be consigned to Drebung, or to Sera, three miles north of Lhasa.

At last the week drew to an end. My kites were taken from me and given away; my bows and beautifully feathered arrows were broken to signify that I was no longer a child and had no use for such things. I felt that my heart, too, was being broken, but no one seemed to think that important.

At nightfall father sent for me and I went to his room, with its wonderful decorations, and the old and valuable books lining the walls. He sat by the side of the main altar, which was in his room, and bade me kneel before him. This was to be the Ceremony of the Opening of the Book. In this large volume, some three feet wide by twelve inches long, were recorded all the details of our family for centuries past. It gave the names of the first of our line, and gave details of the deeds which caused them to be raised to the nobility. Recorded here were the services we had done for our country and for our Ruler. Upon the old, yellowed pages I read history. Now, for the second time, the Book was open for me. First it had been to record my conception and birth. Here were the details upon which the astrologers based their forecasts. Here were the actual charts prepared at the time. Now I had to sign the Book myself, for tomorrow a new life for me would start when I entered the lamasery.

The heavy carved wooden covers were slowly replaced. The golden clasps pressing the thick, hand-made sheets of juniper paper were clipped on. The Book was heavy, even father staggered a little beneath its weight as he rose to replace it in the golden casket which was its protection. Reverently he turned to lower the casket into the deep stone recess beneath the altar. Over a small silver brazier he heated wax, poured it upon the stone lid of the recess, and impressed his seal, so that the Book would not be disturbed.

He turned to me and settled himself comfortably on his cushions. A touch of a gong at his elbow, and a servant brought him buttered tea. There was a long silence, and then he told me of the secret history of Tibet; history going back thousands and thousands of years, a story which was old before the Flood. He told me of the time when Tibet had been washed by an ancient sea, and of how excavations had proved it. Even now, he said, anyone digging near Lhasa could bring to light fossilized sea-animals and strange shells. There were artefacts, too, of strange metal and unknown purpose. Often monks who visited certain caves in the district would discover them and bring them to father. He showed me some. Then his mood changed.

"Because of the Law, to the high-born shall be shown austerity, while to the low shall be shown compassion," he said. "You will undergo a severe ordeal before you are permitted to enter the lamasery." He enjoined upon me the utter necessity of implicit obedience to all commands which would be given to me. His concluding remarks were not conducive to a good night's sleep; he said: "My son, you think I am hard and uncaring, but I care only for the name of the family. I say to you: if you fail in this test for entry, do not return here. You will be as a stranger to this household." With that, with no further word, he motioned me to leave him.

Earlier in the evening I had said my farewells to my sister Yaso. She had been upset, for we had played together so often and she was now but nine years of age, while I would be seven—tomorrow. Mother was not to be found. She had gone to bed and I was not able to say good-bye to her. I made my lonely way to my own room for the last time and arranged the cushions which formed my bed. I lay down, but not to sleep. For a very long time I lay there thinking of the things my father had told me that night. Thinking of the strong dislike father had for children, and thinking of the dreaded morrow when for the first time I would sleep away from home. Gradually the moon moved across the sky. Outside a night bird fluttered on the window sill. From the roof above came the flap-flap of prayer-flags slapping against bare wooden poles. I fell asleep, but as the first feeble rays of the sun replaced the light of the moon, I was awakened by a servant and given a bowl of tsampa and a cup of buttered tea. As I was eating this meagre fare, Tzu bustled into the room. "Well, boy," he said, "our ways part. Thank goodness for that. Now I can go back to my horses. But acquit yourself well; remember all that I have taught you." With that he turned upon his heel and left the room.

Although I did not appreciate it at the time, this was the kindest method. Emotional farewells would have made it very much more difficult for me to leave home—for the first time, for ever, as I thought. If mother had been up to see me off then no doubt I should have tried to persuade her to allow me to remain at home. Many Tibetan children have quite soft lives, mine was hard by any standard, and the lack of farewells, as I later found, was on father's order, so that I should learn discipline and firmness early in life.

I finished my breakfast, tucked my tsampa bowl and cup into the front of my robe, and rolled a spare robe and a pair of felt boots into a bundle. As I crossed the room a servant bade me go softly and not waken the sleeping household. Down the corridor I went. The false dawn had been replaced by the darkness that comes before the true dawn as I made my way down the steps and on to the road. So I left my home. Lonely, frightened, and sick at heart.

CHAPTER FOUR

AT THE TEMPLE GATES

THE road led straight ahead to Chakpori Lamasery, the Temple of Tibetan Medicine. A hard school, this! I walked the miles as the day grew lighter and at the gate leading to the entrance compound I met two others, who also desired admission. We warily looked each other over, and I think that none of us was much impressed by what we saw in the others. We decided that we would have to be sociable if we were going to endure the same training.

For some time we knocked timidly, and nothing happened. Then one of the others stooped and picked up a large stone and really did make enough noise to attract attention. A monk appeared, waving a stick which to our frightened eyes looked as large as a young tree. "What do you young devils want?" he exclaimed. "Do you think that I have nothing better to do than answer the door to such as you?" "We want to be monks," I replied. "You look more like monkeys to me," he said. "Wait there and do not move, the Master of the Acolytes will see you when he is ready." The door slammed shut, nearly knocking one of the other boys flat on his back, he having moved incautiously near. We sat upon the ground, our legs were tired with standing. People came to the lamasery, and went. The pleasant smell of food was wafted to us through a small window, tantalizing us with the thought of satisfying our growing hunger. Food, so near, yet so utterly unattainable.

At last the door was flung open with violence, and a tall, skinny man appeared in the opening. "Well!" he roared. "And what do you miserable scamps want?" "We want to be monks," we said. "Goodness me," he exclaimed. "What garbage is coming to the lamasery nowadays!" He beckoned us to enter the vast walled enclosure which was the perimeter of the lamasery grounds. He asked us what we were, who we were, even *why* we were! We gathered, without difficulty, that he was not at all impressed with us. To one, the son of a herdsman, he said: "Enter quickly, if you can pass your tests you can stay." To the next: "You, boy. *What* did you say? Son of a butcher? A cutter-up of flesh? A transgressor of the Laws of Buddha? And you come here? Be off with you, quickly, or I will have you flogged round the road." The poor wretched boy forgot his tiredness in a sudden burst of speed as the monk lunged at him. Wheeling in a flash he leaped forward, leaving little scuffs of disturbed dust as his feet touched the ground in his hurry.

Now I was left, alone on my seventh birthday. The gaunt monk turned his fierce gaze in my direction, almost causing me to shrivel on the spot with fright. He twitched his stick menacingly "And you? What have we here? Oho! A young prince who wants to turn religious. We must see what you are made of first, my fine fellow. See what kind of stuffing you have; this is not the place for soft and pampered princelings. Take forty paces backwards and sit in the attitude of contemplation until I tell you otherwise, and *do not move an eyelash!*" With that he turned abruptly and went away. Sadly I picked up my pathetic little bundle, and took the forty steps back. On my knees I went, then sat cross-legged as commanded. So I sat throughout the day. Unmoving. The dust blew against me, forming little mounds in the cups of my upturned hands, piling on my shoulders and lodging in my hair. As the sun began to fade my hunger increased and my throat was wracked with the harshness of thirst, for I had had no food or drink since the first light of dawn. Passing monks, and there were many, took no heed. Wandering dogs paused a while to sniff curiously, then they too went away. A gang of small boys came past. One idly flipped a stone in my direction. It struck the side of my head and caused the blood to flow. But I did not stir. I was afraid to. If I failed my endurance test my father would not allow me to enter what had been my home. There was nowhere for me to go. Nothing that I could do. I could only remain motionless, aching in every muscle, stiff in every joint.

The sun hid behind the mountains and the sky became dark. The stars shone bright against the blackness of the sky. From the lamasery windows thousands of little butter lamps flickered into flame. A chill wind, the leaves of the willows hissed and rattled, and about me there were all the faint sounds which go to make the strange noises of the night.

I still remained motionless for the strongest of reasons. I was too frightened to move and I was very stiff. Presently came the soft sush-sush of approaching monks' sandals slithering over the gritty way; the steps of an old man feeling his way in the darkness. A form loomed up before me, the form of an old monk bent and gnarled with the passage of austere years. His hands shook with age, a matter of some concern to me when I saw that he was spilling the tea he was carrying in one hand. In the other hand he held a small bowl of tsampa. He passed them to me. At first I made no move to take them. Divining my thoughts, he said: "Take them, my son, for you can move during the hours of darkness." So I drank the tea and transferred the tsampa to my own bowl. The old monk said, "Now sleep, but at the first rays of the sun take your stance here in the same position, for this is a test, and is not the wanton cruelty which you may now consider it to be. Only those who pass this test can aspire to the higher ranks of our Order." With that he gathered up the cup and the bowl and went away. I stood and stretched my legs, then lay upon my side and finished the tsampa. Now I was really tired, so scooping a depression in the ground to accomodate my hip bone, and placing my spare robe beneath my head, I lay down.

My seven years had not been easy years. At all times father had been strict, frightfully strict, but even so this was my first night away from home and the whole day had been spent in one position, hungry, thirsty, and motionless. I had no idea of what the morrow would bring, or what more would be demanded of me. But now I had to sleep alone beneath the frosty sky, alone with my terror of the darkness, alone with my terrors of the days to come.

It seemed that I had hardly closed my eyes before the sound of a trumpet awakened me. Opening my eyes, I saw that it was the false dawn, with the first light of the approaching day reflected against the skies behind the mountains. Hurriedly I sat up and resumed the posture of contemplation. Gradually the lamasery ahead of me awoke to life. First there had been the air of a sleeping town, a dead, inert hulk. Next, a gentle sighing, as of a sleeper awakening. It grew to a murmur and developed to a deep hum, like the drone of bees on a hot summer's day. Occasionally there was the call of a trumpet, like the muted chirp of a distant bird, and the deep growl of a conch, like a bullfrog calling in a marsh. As the light increased, little groups of shaven heads passed and repassed behind the open windows, windows which in the earlier pre-dawn light had looked like the empty eye-sockets of a clean-picked skull.

The day grew older, and I grew stiffer, but I dared not move; I dared not fall asleep, for if I moved, and failed my test, then I had nowhere to go. Father had made it very clear that if the lamasery did not want me, then nor did he. Little groups of monks came out of the various buildings, going about their mysterious businesses. Small boys wandered around, sometimes kicking a shower of dust and small stones in my direction, or making ribald remarks. As there was no response from me they soon tired of the abortive sport and went away in search of more co-operative victims. Gradually, as the light at eventide began to fail, the little butter-lamps again flickered into life within the lamasery buildings. Soon the darkness was relieved merely by the faint star-glow, for this was the time when the moon rose late. In our saying, the moon was now young and could not travel fast.

I became sick with apprehension; was I forgotten? Was this another test, one in which I had to be deprived of all food? Throughout the long day I had not stirred, and now I was faint with hunger. Suddenly hope flared in me, and I almost jumped to my feet. There was a shuffling noise and a dark outline approached. Then I saw that it was a very large black mastiff dragging something along. He took no notice of me, but went on his nocturnal mission quite uncaring of my plight. My hopes fell; I could have wept. To prevent myself being so weak I reminded myself that only girls and women were as stupid as that.

At last I heard the old man approaching. This time he gazed more benignly upon me and said: "Food and drink, my son, but the end is not yet. There is still the morrow, so take care that you do not move, for so very many fail at the eleventh hour." With those words he turned and went away. While he was speaking I had drunk the tea, and again transferred the tsampa to my own bowl. Again I lay down, certainly no happier than the night before. As I lay there I wondered at the injustice of it; I did not want to be a monk of any sect, shape, or size. I had no more choice than a pack animal being driven over a mountain pass. And so I fell asleep.

The next day, the third day, as I sat in my attitude of contemplation, I could feel myself becoming weaker, and giddy. The lamasery seemed to swim in a miasma compounded of buildings, bright coloured lights, purple patches, with mountains and monks liberally interspersed. With a determined effort I managed to shake off this attack of vertigo. It really frightened me to think that I might fail now, after all the suffering I had had. By now the stones beneath me seemed to have grown knife edges which chafed me in inconvenient places. In one of my lighter moments I thought how glad I was that I was not a hen hatching eggs, and compelled to sit even longer than I.

The sun seemed to stand still; the day appeared endless, but at long last the light began to fail, and the evening wind commenced to play with a feather dropped by a passing bird. Once again the little lights appeared in the windows, one by one. "Hope I die tonight," I thought; "can't stick any more of this." Just then the tall figure of the Master of the Acolytes appeared in the distant doorway. "Boy, come here!" he called. Trying to rise with my stiffened legs, I pitched forward on to my face. "Boy, if you want a rest you can stay there another night. I shall not wait longer." Hastily I grabbed my bundle and tottered towards him. "Enter," he said, "and attend evening service, then see me in the morning."

It was warm inside, and there was the comforting smell of incense. My hunger-sharpened senses told me there was food quite near, so I followed a crowd moving to the right. Food— tsampa, buttered tea. I edged my way to the front row as if I had had a lifetime of practice. Monks made ineffectual grabs at my pigtail as I scrambled between their legs, but I was after *food* and nothing was going to stop me now.

Feeling a little better with some food inside me, I followed the crowd to the inner temple and the evening service. I was too tired to know anything about it, but no one took any notice of me. As the monks filed out I slipped behind a giant pillar, and stretched out on the stone floor, with my bundle beneath my head. I slept.

A stunning crash—I thought my head had split—and the sound of voices. "New boy. One of the high-born. Come on, let's scrag him!" One of the crowd of acolytes was waving my spare robe, which he had pulled from under my head, another had my felt boots. A soft, squashy mass of tsampa caught me in the face. Blows and kicks were rained upon me, but I did not resist, thinking it might be part of the test, to see if I obeyed the sixteenth of the Laws, which ordered: Bear suffering and distress with patience and meekness. There was a sudden loud bellow: "What's going on here?" A frightened whisper: "Oh! It's old Rattlebones on the prowl." As I clawed the tsampa from my eyes the Master of the Acolytes reached down and dragged me to my feet by my pigtail. "Softly! Weakling! *You* one of the future leaders? Bah! Take that, and that!" Blows, hard ones, absolutely showered upon me. "Worthless weakling, can't even defend yourself!" The blows seemed non-ending. I fancied I heard Old Tzu's farewell saying: "Acquit yourself, well, *remember all I have taught you.*" Unthinkingly I turned, and applied a little pressure as Tzu had taught me. The Master was caught by surprise and with a gasp of pain he flew over my head, hit the stone floor, and skidded along on his nose, taking all the skin off, and coming to rest when his head hit a stone pillar with a loud "*onk!*" "Death for me," I thought, "this is the end of all my worries." The world seemed to stand still. The other boys were holding their breath. With a loud roar the tall, bony monk leaped to his feet, blood streaming from his nose. He was roaring all right, roaring with laughter. "Young gamecock, eh? Or cornered rat; which? Ah, that's what we must find out!" Turning and pointing to a tall, ungainly boy of fourteen, he said: "You, Ngawang, you are the biggest bully in this lamasery; see if the son of a yak-driver is better than the son of a prince when it comes to fighting."

For the first time I was grateful to Tzu, the old police monk. In his younger days he had been a champion judo* expert of Kham. He had taught me—as he said—"all he knew". I had had to fight with fully grown men, and in this science, where strength or age does not count, I had become very proficient indeed. Now that I knew that my future depended on the result of this fight, I was at last quite happy.

Nhawang was a strong and well-built boy, but very ungainly in his movements. I could see that he was used to rough-and-tumble fighting, where his strength was in his favour. He rushed at me, intending to grip me and make me helpless. I was not frightened now, thanks to Tzu and his, at times, brutal training. As Ngawang rushed, I moved aside and lightly twisted his arm. His feet skidded from under him, he turned a half-circle and landed on his head. For a moment he lay groaning, then sprang to his feet and leapt at me. I sank to the ground and twisted a leg as he passed over me. This time he spun around and landed on his left shoulder. Still he was not satisfied. He circled warily, then jumped aside and grasped a heavy incense burner which he swung at me by its chains. Such a weapon is slow, cumbersome, and very easy to avoid. I stepped beneath his flailing arms, and lightly stabbed a finger to the base of his neck, as Tzu had so often showed me. Down he went, like a rock on a mountainside, his nerveless fingers relinquishing their grip on the chains, and causing the censer to plummet like a sling-shot at the group of watching boys and monks.

Ngawang was unconscious for about half an hour. That special "touch" is often used to free the spirit from the body for astral travelling and similar purposes.

* The Tibetan system is different and more advanced, but I shall call it "judo" in this book as the Tibetan name would convey nothing to Western readers. See also pp. 95-6.

The Master of the Acolytes stepped forward to me, gave me a slap on the back which almost sent me flat on my face, and made the somewhat contradictory statement: "Boy, you are a man!" My greatly daring reply was: "Then have I earned some food, sir, please? I have had very little of late." "My boy, eat and drink your fill, then tell one of these hooligans—you are their master now—to show you to me."

The old monk who had brought me food before I entered the lamasery came and spoke to me: "My son, you have done well, Ngawang was the bully of the acolytes. Now you take his place and control with kindness and compassion. You have been taught well, see that your knowledge is used well, and does not fall into the wrong hands. Now come with me and I will get you food and drink."

The Master of the Acolytes greeted me amiably when I went to his room. "Sit, boy, sit. I am going to see if your educational prowess is as good as your physical. I am going to try to catch you, boy, so watch out!" He asked me an amazing number of questions, some oral, some written. For six hours we sat opposite each other on our cushions, then he expressed himself as satisfied. I felt like a badly tanned yak-hide, soggy and limp. He stood up. "Boy," he said, "follow me. I am going to take you to the Lord Abbot. An unusual honour, but you will learn why. Come."

Through the wide corridors I followed him, past the religious offices, past the inner temples, and the school rooms. Up the stairs, through more winding corridors, past the Halls of the Gods, and the storage places of herbs. Up more stairs, until, at last, we emerged on the flat roof and walked towards the Lord Abbot's house which was built upon it. Then through the gold-panelled doorway, past the golden Buddha, round by the Symbol of Medicine, and into the Lord Abbot's private room. "Bow, boy, bow, and do as I do. Lord, here is the boy Tuesday Lobsang Rampa." With that, the Master of the Acolytes bowed three times, then prostrated himself upon the floor. I did the same, panting with eagerness to do the right thing in the right way. The impassive Lord Abbot looked at us and said: "Sit." We sat upon cushions, cross-legged, in the Tibetan way.

For a long time the Lord Abbot remained looking at me, but not speaking. Then he said: "Tuesday Lobsang Rampa, I know all about you, all that has been predicted. Your trial of endurance has been harsh but with good reason. That reason you will know in later years. Know now that of every thousand monks, only one is fitted for higher things, for higher development. The others drift, and do their daily task. They are the manual workers, those who turn the prayer-wheels without wondering why. We are not short of them, we *are* short of those who will carry on our knowledge when later our country is under an alien cloud. You will be specially trained, intensively trained, and in a few short years you will be given more knowledge than a lama normally acquires in a long lifetime. The Way will be hard, and often it will be painful. To force clairvoyance is painful, and to travel in the astral planes requires nerves that nothing can shatter, and a determination as hard as the rocks."

I listened hard, taking it all in. It all seemed too difficult to me. I was not that energetic! He went on: "You will be trained here in medicine and in astrology. You will be given every assistance which we can render. You will also be trained in the esoteric arts. Your Path is mapped for you, Tuesday Lobsang Rampa. Although you are but seven years of age, I speak to you as a man, for thus

you have been brought up." He inclined his head, and the Master of the Acolytes rose and bowed deeply. I did the same, and together we made our way out. Not until we were again in the Master's room did he break the silence. "Boy, you will have to work hard all the time. But we will help you all we can. Now I will have you taken to get your head shaved." In Tibet, when a boy enters the priesthood, his head is shaved with the exception of one lock. This lock is removed when the boy is given the "priest-name", and his former name is discarded, but more of that a little further on.

The Master of the Acolytes led me through winding ways to a small room, the "barber shop". Here I was told to sit on the floor. "Tam-chö," the Master said, "shave this boy's head. Remove the name lock as well, for he is being given his name immediately." Tam-chö stepped forward, grasped my pigtail in his right hand and lifted it straight up. "Ah! my boy. Lovely pigtail, well buttered, well cared for. A pleasure to saw it off." From somewhere he produced a huge pair of shears—the sort our servants used for cutting plants. "Tishe," he roared, "come and hold up this end of rope." Tishe, the assistant, came running forward and held up my pigtail so tightly that I was almost lifted off the ground. With his tongue protruding, and with many little grunts, Tam-chö manipulated those deplorably blunt shears, until my pigtail was severed. This was just the start. The assistant brought a bowl of hot water, so hot that I jumped off the floor in anguish when it was poured on my head. "What's the matter, boy? Being boiled?" I replied that I was, and he said: "Never mind that, it makes the hair easier to remove!" He took up a three-sided razor, very like the thing we had at home for scraping floors. Eventually, after an eternity, it seemed to me, my head was denuded of hair.

"Come with me," said the Master. He led me to his room and produced a big book. "Now, what are we to call you?" He went on mumbling to himself, then, "Ah! here we are: from now on you will be called Yza-mig-dmar Lah-lu." For this book, however, I shall continue to use the name of Tuesday Lobsang Rampa, as it is easier for the reader.

Feeling as naked as a new-laid egg, I was taken to a class. Having had such a good education at home, I was considered to know more than the average, so was put in the class of the seventeen-year-old acolytes. I felt like a dwarf among giants. The others had seen how I had handled Ngawang, so I had no trouble except for the incident of one big, stupid boy. He came up behind me and put his dirty great hands on my very sore pate. It was just a matter of reaching up and jabbing my fingers into the ends of his elbows to send him away screaming with pain. Try knocking two "funny bones" at once, and see! Tzu really taught me well. The judo instructors whom I was to meet later in the week all knew Tzu; all said he was the finest "judo adept" in the whole of Tibet. I had no more trouble from boys. Our teacher, who had had his back turned when the boy put his hands on my head, had soon noticed what was happening. He laughed so much at the result that he let us go early.

It was now about eight-thirty in the evening, so we had about three-quarters of an hour to spare before temple service at nine-fifteen. My joy was short-lived; as we were leaving the room a lama beckoned to me. I went to him and he said: "Come with me." I followed him, wondering what fresh trouble was in store. He turned into a music room where there were about twenty boys whom I knew to be entrants like myself. Three musicians sat at their instruments, one at a drum, one had a conch, and the other a silver trumpet. The lama said: "We will sing so that I may test your voices for the choir," The musicians started, playing a very well-known air which everyone could sing. We raised our voices. The Music Master raised his eyebrows. The puzzled look on his face was replaced by one of real pain. Up went his two hands in protest. "Stop! Stop!" he shouted, "even the Gods must writhe at this. Now start again and *do it properly*." We started again. Again we were stopped. This time the Music Master came straight to me. "Dolt," he exclaimed, "you are trying to make fun of me. We will have the musicians play, and you sing alone as you will not sing in company!" Once again the music started. Once again I raised my voice in song. But not for long. The Music Master waved to me in a frenzy. "Tuesday Lobsang, your talents do *not* include music. Never in my fifty-five years here have I heard such an off-key voice. Off-key? It is no key at all! Boy, you will not sing again. In the singing sessions you will study other things. In the temple services you will not sing, or your disharmony will ruin all. Now go, you unmusical vandal!" I went.

I idled around until I heard the trumpets announcing that it was time to assemble for the last service. Last night —good gracious— was it only *last* night that I had entered the lamasery? It seemed ages. I felt that I was walking in my sleep, and I was hungry again. Perhaps that was just as well, if I had been full I should have dropped off to sleep. Someone grabbed my robe, and I was swung up in the air. A huge, friendly looking lama had hoisted me up to his broad shoulder. "Come on, boy, you will be late for service, and then you'll catch it. You miss your supper, you know, if you are late, and you feel as empty as a drum." He entered the temple still carrying me and took his place just at the back of the boys' cushions. Carefully he placed me on a cushion in front of him. "Face me, boy, and make the same responses as I do, but when I sing, *you*—ha! ha!—keep quiet." I was indeed grateful for his help, so few people had ever been kind to me; instruction I had had in the past had been yelled in one end, or knocked in the other.

I must have dozed, because I came to with a start to find that the service had ended, and the big lama had carried me, asleep, to the refectory and put tea, tsampa, and some boiled vegetables in front of me. "Eat it up, boy, then get off to bed. I'll show you where to sleep. For this night you can sleep until five in the morning, then come to me." That is the last thing I heard until at five in the morning I was awakened, with difficulty, by a boy who had been friendly the day before. I saw that I was in a large room, and was resting on three cushions. "The Lama Mingyar Dondup told me to see that you were awakened at five." Up I got and piled my cushions against a wall as I saw the others had done. The others were moving out, and the boy with me said: "We must hurry for breakfast, then I have to take you to the Lama Mingyar Dondup." Now I was becoming more settled, not that I liked the place, or wanted to stay. But it did occur to me that as I had no choice whatever, I should be my own best friend if I settled without any fuss.

At breakfast, the Reader was droning out something from one of the hundred and twelve volumes of the Kan-gyur, the Buddhist Scriptures. He must have seen that I was thinking of something else, for he rapped out: "*You*, small new boy there, what did I say last? Quick!" Like a flash, and quite without thinking, I replied: "Sir, you said 'that boy is not listening, I'll catch him'!" That certainly raised a laugh and saved me from a hiding for inattention. The Reader smiled—a rare event—and explained that he had asked for the text from the Scriptures, but I could "get away with it this time".

At all meals Readers stand at a lectern and read from sacred books. Monks are not allowed to talk at meals, nor to think of food. They must ingest sacred knowledge with their food. We all sat on the floor, on cushions, and ate from a table which was about eighteen inches high. We were not permitted to make any noise at meal times, and we were absolutely banned from resting our elbows on the table.

The discipline at Chakpori was indeed iron. Chakpori means "Iron Mountain". In most lamaseries there was little organized discipline or routine. Monks could work or laze as they pleased. Perhaps one in a thousand wanted to make progress, and they were the ones who became lamas, for lama means "superior one" and is not applied to all and sundry. In our lamasery the discipline was strict, even fiercely so. We were going to be specialists, leaders of our class, and for us order and training was considered to be utterly essential. We boys were not allowed to use the normal white robes of an acolyte, but had to wear the russet of the accepted monk. We had domestic workers as well, but these monks were servant-monks who saw to the housekeeping side of the lamasery. We had to take turns at domestic work to make sure that we did not get exalted ideas. We always had to remember the old Buddhist saying: "Being yourself the example, do only good, and no harm, to others. This is the essence of Buddha's teaching." Our Lord Abbot, the Lama Cham-pa La, was as strict as my father, and demanded instant obedience. One of his sayings was: "Reading and writing are the gates of all qualities", so we got plenty to do in that line.

CHAPTER FIVE

LIFE AS A CHELA

OUR "day" started at midnight at Chakpori. As the midnight trumpet sounded, echoing through the dimly lit corridors, we would roll sleepily off our bed-cushions and fumble in the darkness for our robes. We all slept in the nude, the usual system in Tibet where there is no false modesty. With our robes on, off we would go, tucking our belongings into the pouched-up front of our dress. Down the passageways we would clatter, not in a good mood at that hour. Part of our teaching was: "It is better to rest with a peaceful mind than to sit like Buddha and pray when angry." My irreverent thought often was: "Well, why can't *we* rest with a peaceful mind? This midnight stunt makes *me* angry!" But no one gave me a satisfactory answer, and I had to go with the others into the Prayer Hall. Here the innumerable butter-lamps struggled to shed their rays of light through the drifting clouds of incense smoke. In the flickering light, with the shifting shadows, the giant sacred figures seemed to become alive, to bow and sway in response to our chants.

The hundreds of monks and boys would sit cross-legged on cushions on the floor. All would sit in rows the length of the hall. Each pair or rows would face each other so that the first and second rows would be face to face, the second and third would be back to back, and so on. We would have our chants and sacred songs which employ special tonal scales because in the East it is realized that sounds have power. Just as a musical note can shatter

58

a glass, so can a combination of notes build up metaphysical power. There would also be readings from the Kan-gyur. It was a most impressive sight to see these hundreds of men in blood-red robes and golden stoles, swaying and chanting in unison, with the silver tinkle of little bells, and the throbbing of drums. Blue clouds of incense smoke coiled and wreathed about the knees of the gods, and every so often it seemed, in the uncertain light, that one or other of the figures was gazing straight at us.

The service would last about an hour, then we would return to our sleeping-cushions until four in the morning. Another service would start at about four-fifteen. At five we would have our first meal, of tsampa and buttered tea. Even at this meal the Reader would be droning out his words, and the Disciplinarian would be watchful at his side. At this meal any special orders or information would be given. It might be that something was wanted from Lhasa, and then at the breakfast meal the names of the monks would be called, those who were going to take or collect the goods. They would also be given special dispensation to be away from the lamasery for such and such a time, and to miss a certain number of services.

At six o'clock we would be assembled in our classrooms ready for the first session of our studies. The second of our Tibetan Laws was: "You shall perform religious observances, and study." In my seven-year-old ignorance I could not understand why we had to obey that Law, when the fifth Law, "You shall honour your elders, and *those of high birth*", was flaunted and broken. All my experience had led me to believe that there was something shameful in being of "high birth". Certainly I had been victimized for it. It did not occur to me then that it is not the rank of birth that matters, but the character of the person concerned.

We attended another service at nine in the morning, interrupting our studies for about forty minutes. Quite a welcome break, sometimes, but we had to be in class again by a quarter to ten. A different subject was started then, and we had to work at it until one o'clock. Still we were not free to eat; a half-hour service came first and then we had our buttered tea and tsampa. One hour of manual labour followed, to give us exercise and to teach us humility. I seemed more often than not to collect the messiest of most unpleasant type of job.

Three o'clock saw us trooping off for an hour of enforced rest; we were not allowed to talk or move, but just had to lie still. This was not a popular time because the hour was too short for a sleep and too long to stay idle. We could think of much better things to do! At four, after this rest, we returned to our studies. This was the dreaded period of the day, five hours without a break, five hours when we could not leave the room for anything without incurring the severest penalties. Our teachers were quite free with their stout canes and some of them tackled the punishment of offenders with real enthusiasm. Only the badly pressed or most foolhardy pupils asked to "be excused" when punishment on one's return was inevitable.

Our release came at nine o'clock when we had the last meal of the day. Again this was buttered tea and tsampa. Sometimes—only sometimes—we had vegetables. Usually that meant sliced turnips, or some very small beans. They were raw, but to hungry boys they were very acceptable. On one unforgettable occasion, when I was eight, we had some pickled walnuts. I was particularly fond of them, having had them often at home. Now, foolishly, I tried to work an exchange with another boy: he to have my spare robe in exchange for his pickled walnuts. The Disciplinarian heard, and I was called to the middle of the hall and made to confess my sin. As a punishment for "greediness" I had to remain without food or drink for twenty-four hours. My spare robe was taken from me as it was said that I had no use for it, "having been willing to barter it for that which was not essential".

At nine-thirty we went to our sleeping-cushions, "bed" to us. No one was late for bed! I thought the long hours would kill me, I thought that I should drop dead at any moment, or that I would fall asleep and never again awaken. At first I, and the other new boys, used to hide in corners for a good doze. After quite a short time I became used to the long hours and took no notice at all of the length of the day.

It was just before six in the morning when, with the help of the boy who had awakened me, I found myself in front of the Lama Mingyar Dondup's door. Although I had not knocked, he called for me to enter. His room was a very pleasant one and there were wonderful wall paintings, some of them actually painted on the walls and others painted on silk and hanging. A few small statuettes were on low tables, they were of gods and goddesses and were made of jade, gold, and cloisonné. A large Wheel of Life also hung upon the wall. The lama was sitting in the lotus attitude on his cushion and before him, on a low table, he had a number of books, one of which he was studying as I entered.

"Sit here with me, Lobsang," he said, "we have a lot of things to discuss together, but first an important question to a growing man: have you had enough to eat and drink?" I assured him that I had. "The Lord Abbot has said that we can work together. We have traced your previous incarnation and it was a good one. Now we want to redevelop certain powers and abilities you then had. In the space of a very few years we want you to have more knowledge than a lama has in a very long life." He paused, and looked at me long and hard. His eyes were very piercing. "All men must be free to choose their own path," he continued, "your way will be hard for forty years, if you take the right path, but it will lead to great benefits in the next life. The wrong path now will give you comforts, softness, and riches in *this* life, but you will not develop. You and you alone can choose." He stopped, and looked at me.

"Sir," I replied, "my father told me that if I failed at the lamasery I was not to return home. How then would I have softness and comfort if I had no home to which to return? And who would show me the right path if I choose it?" He smiled at me and answered: "Have you already forgotten? We have traced your previous incarnation. If you choose the wrong path, the path of softness, you will be installed in a lamasery as a Living Incarnation, and in a very few years will be an abbot in charge. Your father would not call that failure!"

Something in the way he spoke made me ask a further question: "Would *you* consider it a failure?"

"Yes," he replied, "knowing what I know, I would call it a failure."

"And who will show me the way?"

"I will be your guide if you take the right path, but you are the one to choose, no one can influence your decision."

I looked at him, stared at him. And liked what I saw. A big man, with keen black eyes. A broad open face, and a high forehead. Yes, I liked what I saw. Although only seven years of age, I had had a hard life, and met many people, and really could judge if a man was good.

"Sir," I said, "I would like to be your pupil and take the right path." I added somewhat ruefully, I suppose, "But I still don't like hard work!"

He laughed, and his laugh was deep and warming. "Lobsang, Lobsang, *none* of us really like hard work, but few of us are truthful enough to admit it." He looked through his papers. We shall need to do a little operation to your head soon to force clairvoyance, and then we will speed your studies hypnotically. We are going to take you far in metaphysics, as well as in medicine!"

I felt a bit gloomy, more hard work. It seemed to me that I had had to work hard all my seven years, and there seemed to be little play, or kite flying. The lama seemed to know my thoughts. "Oh yes, young man. There will be much kite flying later, the real thing: man-lifters. But first we must map out how best to arrange these studies." He turned to his papers, and riffled through them. "Let me see, nine o'clock until one. Yes, that will do for a start. Come here every day at nine, instead of attending service, and we will see what interesting things we can discuss. Starting from tomorrow. Have you any message for your father and mother? I'm seeing them today. Giving them your pigtail!"

I was quite overcome. When a boy was accepted by a lamasery his pigtail was cut off and his head shaved, the pigtail would be sent to the parents, carried by a small acolyte, as a symbol that their son had been accepted. Now the Lama Mingyar Dondup was taking my pigtail to deliver in person. That meant that he had accepted me as his own personal charge, as his "spiritual son". This lama was a very important man, a very clever man, one who had a most enviable reputation throughout Tibet. I knew that I could not fail under such a man.

That morning, back in the classroom, I was a most inattentive pupil. My thoughts were elsewhere, and the teacher had ample time and opportunity to satisfy his joy in punishing at least one small boy!

It all seemed very hard, the severity of the teachers. But then, I consoled myself, that is why I came, to learn. That is why I reincarnated, although then I did not remember what it was that I had to relearn. We firmly believe in reincarnation, in Tibet. We believe that when one reaches a certain advanced stage of evolution, one can choose to go on to another plane of existence, or return to earth to learn something more, or to help others. It may be that a wise man had a certain mission in life, but died before he could complete his work. In that case, so we believe, he can return to complete his task, providing that the result will be of benefit to others. Very few people could have their previous incarnations traced back, there had to be certain signs and the cost and time would prohibit it. Those who had those signs, as I had, were termed "Living Incarnations". They were subjected to the sternest of stern treatment when they were young—as I had been—but became objects of reverence when they became older. In my case I was going to have special treatment to "force-feed" my occult knowledge. Why, I did not know, then!

A rain of blows on my shoulders brought me back to the reality of the classroom with a violent jerk. "Fool, dolt, imbecile! Have the mind demons penetrated your thick skull? It is more than I could do. You are fortunate that it is now time to attend service." With that remark, the enraged teacher gave me a final hearty blow, for good measure, and stalked out of the room. The boy next to me said, "Don't forget, it's our turn to work in the kitchens this afternoon. Hope we get a chance to fill our tsampa bags." Kitchen work was hard, the "regulars" there used to treat us boys as slaves. There was no hour of rest for us after kitchen hour. Two solid hours of hard labour, then straight to the classroom again. Sometimes we would be kept later in the kitchens, and so be late for class. A fuming teacher would be waiting for us, and would lay about him with his stick without giving us any opportunity of explaining the reason.

My first day of work in the kitchens was nearly my last. We trooped reluctantly along the stone-flagged corridors towards the kitchens. At the door we were met by an angry monk: "Come on, you lazy, useless rascals," he shouted. "The first ten of you, get in there and stoke the fires." I was the tenth. Down another flight of steps we went. The heat was overpowering. In front of us we saw a ruddy light, the light of roaring fires. Huge piles of yak-dung lay about, this was fuel for the furnaces. "Get those iron scoops and stoke for your lives," the monk in charge yelled. I was just a poor seven-year-old among the others of my class, among whom was none younger than seventeen. I could scarcely lift the scoop, and in straining to put the fuel in the fire I tipped it over the monk's feet. With a roar of rage he seized me by the throat, swung me round—and tripped. I was sent flying backwards. A terrible pain shot through me, and there was the sickening smell of burning flesh. I had fallen against the red-hot end of a bar protruding from the furnace. I fell with a scream to the floor, among the hot ashes. At the top of my left leg, almost at the leg joint, the bar had burned its way in until stopped by the bone. I still have the dead-white scar, which even now causes me some trouble. By this scar I was in later years to be identified by the Japanese.

There was uproar. Monks came rushing from everywhere. I was still among the hot ashes but was soon lifted out. Quite a lot of my body had superficial burns, but the leg burn really was serious. Quickly I was carried upstairs to a lama. He was a medical lama, and applied himself to the task of saving my leg. The iron had been rusty, and when it entered my leg, flakes of rust had remained behind. He had to probe round and scoop out the pieces until the wound was clean. Then it was tightly packed with a powdered herb compress. The rest of my body was dabbed with a herbal lotion which certainly eased the pain of the fire. My leg was throbbing and throbbing and I was sure that I would never walk again. When he had finished, the lama called a monk to carry me to a small side-room, where I was put to bed on cushions. An old monk came in and sat on the floor beside me and started muttering prayers over me. I thought to myself that it was a fine thing to offer prayers for my safety *after* the accident had happened. I also decided to lead a good life, as I now had personal experience of what it felt like when the fire devils tormented one. I thought of a picture I had seen, in which a devil was prodding an unfortunate victim in much the same place as I had been burned.

It may be thought that monks were terrible people, not at all what one would expect. But—"monks"—what does it mean? We understand that word as anyone, male, living in the lamastic service. Not necessarily a religious person. In Tibet almost anyone can become a monk. Often a boy is "sent to be a monk" without having any choice at all in the matter. Or a man may decide that he has had enough of sheep herding, and wants to be sure of a roof over his head when the temperature is forty below zero. He becomes a monk not through religious convictions, but for his own creature comfort. The lamaseries had "monks" as their domestic staff, as their builders, labourers, and scavengers. In other parts of the world they would be termed "servants" or the equivalent. Most of them had had a hard time; life at twelve to twenty thousand feet can be difficult, and often they were hard on us boys just for sheer want of thought or feeling. To us the term "monk" was synonymous with "man". We named the members of the priesthood quite differently. A *chela* was a boy pupil, a novice, or acolyte. Nearest to what the average man means by "monk" is *trappa*. He is the most numerous of those in a lamasery. Then we come to that most abused term, a *lama*. If the trappas are the non-commissioned soldiers, then the lama is the commissioned officer. Judging by the way most people in the West talk and write, there are more officers than men! Lamas are masters, *gurus*, as we term them. The Lama Mingyar Dondup was going to be my guru, and I his chela. After the lamas there were the abbots. Not all of them were in charge of lamaseries, many were engaged in the general duties of senior administration, or travelling from lamasery to lamasery. In some instances, a particular lama could be of higher status than an abbot, it depended upon what he was doing. Those who were "Living Incarnations", such as I had been proved, could be made abbots at the age of fourteen; it depended upon whether they could pass the severe examinations. These groups were strict and stern, but they were not cruel; they were at all times just. A further example of "monks" can be seen in the term "police monks". Their sole purpose was to keep order, they were not concerned with the temple ceremonial except that they had to be present to make sure that everything was orderly. The police monks often were cruel and, as stated, so were the domestic staff. One could not condemn a bishop because his under-gardener misbehaved! Nor expect the under-gardener to be a saint just because he worked for a bishop.

In the lamasery we had a prison. Not by any means a pleasant place to be in, but the characters of those who were consigned to it were not pleasant either. My solitary experience of it was when I had to treat a prisoner who had been taken ill. It was when I was almost ready to leave the lamasery that I was called to the prison cell. Out in the back courtyard were a number of circular parapets, about three feet high. The massive stones forming them were as wide as they were high. Covering the tops were stone bars each as thick as a man's thigh. They covered a circular opening about nine feet across. Four police monks grasped the centre bar, and dragged it aside. One stooped and picked up a yak-hair rope, at the end of which there was a flimsy-looking loop. I looked on unhappily; trust myself to *that*? "Now, Honourable Medical Lama," said the man, "if you will step here and put your foot in this we will lower you." Gloomily I complied. "You will want a light, sir," the police monk said, and passed me a flaring torch made of yarn soaked in butter. My gloom increased; I had to hold on to the rope, and hold the torch, and avoid setting myself on fire or burning through the thin little rope which so dubiously supported me. But down I went, twenty-five or thirty feet, down between walls glistening with water, down to the filthy stone floor. By the light of the torch I saw an evil-looking wretch crouched against the wall. Just one look was enough, there was no aura around him, so no life. I said a prayer for the soul wandering between the planes of existence, and closed the wild, staring eyes, then called to be pulled up. My work was finished, now the body-breakers would take over. I asked what had been his crime, and was told that he had been a wandering beggar who had come to the lamasery for food and shelter, and then, in the night, killed a monk for his few possessions. He had been overtaken while escaping, and brought back to the scene of his crime.

But all that is somewhat of a digression from the incident of my first attempt at kitchen work.

The effects of the cooling lotions were wearing off, and I felt as if the skin were being scorched off my body. The throbbing in my leg increased, it seemed as if it was going to explode; to my fevered imagination the hole was filled with a flaming torch. Time dragged; throughout the lamasery there were sounds, some that I knew, and many that I did not. The pain was sweeping up my body in great fiery gouts. I lay on my face, but the front of my body also was burned, burned by the hot ashes. There was a faint rustle, and someone sat beside me. A kind, compassionate voice, the voice of the Lama Mingyar Dondup said: "Little friend, it is too much. Sleep." Gentle fingers swept along my spine. Again, and again, and I knew no more.

A pale sun was shining in my eyes. I blinked awake, and with the first returning consciousness thought that someone was kicking me—that I had overslept. I tried to jump up, to attend service, but fell back in agony. My leg! A soothing voice spoke: "Keep still, Lobsang, this is a day of rest for you." I turned my head stiffly, and saw with great astonishment that I was in the lama's room, and that he was sitting beside me. He saw my look and smiled. "And why the amazement? Is it not right that two friends should be together when one is sick?" My somewhat faint reply was: "But you are a Head Lama, and I am just a boy."

"Lobsang, we have gone far together in other lives. In this, yet, you do not remember. I do, we were very close together in our last incarnations. But now you must rest and regain your strength. We are going to save your leg for you, so do not worry."

I thought of the Wheel of Existence, I thought of the injunction in our Buddhist Scriptures:

> The prosperity of the generous man never fails, while the miser finds no comforter.
>
> Let the powerful man be generous to the suppliant. Let him look down the long path of lives. For riches revolve like the wheels of a cart, they come now to one, now to another. The beggar today is a prince tomorrow, and the prince may come as a beggar.

It was obvious to me even then that the lama who was now my guide was indeed a good man, and one whom I would follow to the utmost of my ability. It was clear that he knew a very great deal about me, far more than I knew myself. I was looking forward to studying with him, and I resolved that no one should have a better pupil. There was, as I could plainly feel, a very strong affinity between us, and I marvelled at the workings of Fate which had placed me in his care.

I turned my head to look out of the window. My bed-cushions had been placed on a table so that I could see out. It seemed very strange to be resting off the floor, some four feet in the air. My childish fancy likened it to a bird roosting in a tree! But there was much to see. Far away over the lower roofs beneath the window, I could see Lhasa sprawled in the sunlight. Little houses, dwarfed by the distance, and all of delicate pastel shades. The meandering waters of the Kyi River flowed through the level valley, flanked by the greenest of green grass. In the distance the mountains were purple, surmounted with white caps of shining snow. The nearer mountain-sides were speckled with golden-roofed lamaseries. To the left was the Potala with its immense bulk forming a small mountain. Slightly to the right of us was a small wood from which peeped temples and colleges. This was the home of the State Oracle of Tibet, an important gentleman whose sole task in life is to connect the material world with the immaterial. Below, in the forecourt, monks of all ranks were passing to and fro. Some wore a sombre brown robe, these were the worker monks. A small group of boys were wearing white, student monks from some more distant lamasery. Higher ranks were there, too: those in blood red, and those with purple robes. These latter often had golden stoles upon them, indicating that they were connected with the higher administration. A number were on horses or ponies. The laity rode coloured animals, while the priests used only white. But all this was taking me away from the immediate present. I was more concerned now about getting better and being able to move around again.

After three days it was thought better for me to get up and move around. My leg was very stiff and shockingly painful. The whole area was inflamed and there was much discharge caused by the particles of iron rust which had not been removed. As I could not walk unaided, a crutch was made, and I hopped about on this with some resemblance to a wounded bird. My body still had a large number of burns and blisters from the hot ashes, but the whole lot together was not as painful as my leg. Sitting was impossible, I had to lie on my right side or on my face. Obviously I could not attend services or the classrooms, so my Guide, the Lama Mingyar Dondup, taught me almost full time. He expressed himself as well satisfied with the amount I had learnt in my few years, and said, "But a lot of this you have unconsciously remembered from your last incarnation."

CHAPTER SIX

LIFE IN THE LAMASERY

Two weeks went by and my body burns were very much better. My leg was still troublesome but at least it was making progress. I asked if I could resume normal routine as I wanted to be moving about more. It was agreed that I should, but I was given permission to sit in any way I could, or to lie on my face. Tibetans sit cross-legged in what we call the lotus attitude, but my leg disability definitely prevented that.

On the first afternoon of my return there was work in the kitchens. My job was to have a slate and keep check of the number of bags of barley being roasted. The barley was spread out on a stone floor which was smoking hot. Beneath was the furnace at which I had been burned. The barley was evenly distributed, and the door shut. While that lot was roasting we trooped along a corridor to a room where we cracked barley which had previously been roasted. There was a rough stone basin, cone-shaped and about eight feet across at the widest part. The internal surface was grooved and scored to hold grains of barley. A large stone, also cone-shaped, fitted loosely into the basin. It was supported by an age-worn beam which passed through it, and to which were fixed smaller beams like the spokes of a wheel without a rim. Roasted barley was poured into the basin, and monks and boys strained at the spokes to turn the stone, which weighed many tons. Once it started it was not so bad, then we all trooped around singing songs. I could sing here without reprimand! Starting the wretched stone was terrible. Everyone had to lend a hand to get it moving. Then, once moving, great care was taken to see that it did not stop.

Fresh supplies of roasted barley were poured in as the crushed grains dropped out of the bottom of the basin. All the cracked barley was taken away, spread on to hot stones, and roasted again. That was the basis of tsampa. Each of us boys carried a week's supply of tsampa on us or, more correctly, we carried the cracked and roasted barley on us. At meal-times we poured a little of it from our leather bags into our bowls. Then we would add buttered tea, stir with our fingers until the mass was like dough, then we would eat it.

The next day we had to work helping to make tea. We went to another part of the kitchens where there was a cauldron holding a hundred and fifty gallons. This had been scoured out with sand and now gleamed like new metal. Earlier in the day it had been half-filled with water, and this was now boiling and steaming. We had to fetch bricks of tea and crush them up. Each brick was about fourteen to sixteen pounds in weight and had been brought to Lhasa over the mountain passes from China and India. The crushed pieces were tossed into the boiling water. A monk would add a great block of salt, and another would put in an amount of soda. When everything was boiling again, shovelfuls of clarified butter would be added and the whole lot boiled for hours. This mixture had a very good food value and with the tsampa was quite sufficient to sustain life. At all times the tea was kept hot, and as one cauldron became used, another was filled and prepared. The worst part of preparing this tea was tending the fires. The yak-dung which we used instead of wood as fuel is dried into the form of slabs and there is an almost inexhaustible supply of it. When put on the fires it sends out clouds of evil-smelling, acrid smoke. Everything in range of the smoke would gradually become blackened, woodwork would eventually look like ebony, and faces exposed to it for long would become grimed by smoke-filled pores.

We had to help with all this menial work, not because there was a shortage of labour, but so that there should not be too much class distinction. We believe that the only enemy is the man you do not know; work alongside a man, talk to him, know him, and he ceases to be an enemy. In Tibet, on one day in every year, those in authority set aside their powers, and then any subordinate can say exactly what they think. If an abbot has been harsh during the year, he is told about it, and if the criticism is just, no action can be taken against the subordinate. It is a system that works well and is rarely abused. It provides a means of justice against the powerful, and gives the lower ranks a feeling that they have some say after all.

There was a lot to be studied in the classrooms. We sat in rows on the floor. When the teacher was lecturing to us, or writing on his wall-board, he stood in front of us. But when we were working at our lessons, he walked about at the back of us and we had to work hard all the time as we did not know which of us was being watched! He carried a very substantial stick and did not hesitate to use it on any part of us within immediate reach. Shoulders, arms, backs, or the more othodox place—it did not matter at all to the teachers, one place was as good as another.

We studied a lot of mathematics, because that was a subject which was essential for astrological work. Our astrology was no mere hit-or-miss affair, but was worked out according to scientific principles. I had a lot of astrology drummed into me because it was necessary to use it in medical work. It is better to treat a person according to their astrological type than to prescribe something quite haphazardly in the hope that as it once cured a person, it may again. There were large wall charts dealing with astrology, and others showing pictures of various herbs. These latter were changed every week and we were expected to be entirely familiar with the appearance of all the plants. Later we would be taken on excursions to gather and prepare these herbs, but we were not allowed to go on these until we had a far better knowledge and could be trusted to pick the right varieties. These "herb-gathering" expeditions, which were in the fall of the year, were a very popular relaxation from the strict routine of the lamastic life. Sometimes such a visit would last for three months, and would take one to the highlands, an area of ice-bound land, twenty to twenty-five thousand feet above the sea, where the vast ice sheets were interrupted by green valleys heated by hot springs. Here one could have an experience matched perhaps nowhere else in the world. In moving fifty yards one could range from a temperature of forty below zero to a hundred or more, Fahrenheit, above. This area was quite unexplored except by a few of us monks.

Our religious instruction was quite intensive; every morning we had to recite the Laws and Steps of the Middle Way. These Laws were:

1. Have faith in the leaders of the lamasery and country.
2. Perform religious observances, and study hard.
3. Pay honour to the parents.
4. Respect the virtuous.
5. Honour elders and those of high birth.
6. Help one's country.
7. Be honest and truthful in all things.
8. Pay heed to friends and relatives.

9. Make the best use of food and wealth.
10. Follow the example of those who are good.
11. Show gratitude and return kindness.
12. Give fair measure in all things.
13. Be free from jealousy and envy.
14. Refrain from scandal.
15. Be gentle in speech and in action and harm none.
16. Bear suffering and distress with patience and meekness.

We were constantly told that if everyone obeyed those Laws, there would be no strife or disharmony. Our lamasery was noted for its austerity and rigorous training. Quite a number of monks came from other lamaseries and then left in search of softer conditions. We looked upon them as failures and upon ourselves as of the élite. Many other lamaseries had no night services; the monks went to bed at dark and stayed there until dawn. To us they seemed soft and effete, and although we grumbled to ourselves, we would have grumbled still more if our schedule had been altered to bring us to the inefficient level of the others. The first year was particularly hard. Then was the time to weed out those who were failures. Only the strongest could survive on visits to the frozen highlands in search of herbs, and we of Chakpori were the only men to go there. Wisely our leaders decided to eliminate the unsuitable before they could in any way endanger others. During the first year we had almost no relaxation, no amusements and games. Study and work occupied every waking moment.

One of the things for which I am still grateful is the way in which we were taught to memorize. Most Tibetans have good memories, but we who were training to be medical monks had to know the names and exact descriptions of a very large number of herbs, as well as knowing how they could be combined and used. We had to know much about astrology, and be able to recite the whole of our sacred books. A method of memory training had been evolved throughout the centuries. We imagined that we were in a room lined with thousands and thousands of drawers. Each drawer was clearly labelled, and the writing on all the labels could be read with ease from where we stood. Every fact we were told had to be classified, and we were instructed to imagine that we opened the appropriate drawer and put the fact inside. We had to visualize it very clearly as we did it, visualize the "fact" and the exact location of the "drawer". With little practice it was amazingly easy to—in imagination—enter the room, open the correct drawer, and extract the fact required as well as all related facts.

Our teachers went to great pains to ram home the need for good memories. They would shoot questions at us merely to test our

71

memories. The questions would be quite unrelated to each other so that we could not follow a trend and take an easy path. Often it would be questions on obscure pages of the sacred books interspersed with queries about herbs. The punishment for forgetfulness was most severe; forgetting was the unforgivable crime and was punished with a severe beating. We were not given a long time in which to try to remember. The teacher would perhaps say: "You, boy, I want to know the fifth line of the eighteenth page of the seventh volume of the Kan-gyur, open the drawer, now, what is it?" Unless one could answer within about ten seconds it was as well not to answer, because the punishment would be even worse if there was any mistake, no matter how slight. It is a good system, though, and does train the memory. We could not carry books of facts. Our books were usually about three feet wide by about eighteen inches long, loose sheets of paper held unbound between wooden covers. Certainly I found a good memory to be of the utmost value in later years.

During the first twelve months we were not allowed out of the lamasery grounds. Those who did leave were not permitted to return. This was a rule peculiar to Chakpori, because the discipline was so strict it was feared that if we were allowed out we should not return. I admit that I should have "run for it" if I had had anywhere to run. After the first year we were used to it.

The first year we were not permitted to play any games at all, we were kept hard at work the whole time and this most effectively weeded out those who were weak and unable to stand the strain. After these first hard months we found that we had almost forgotten how to play. Our sports and exercises were designed to toughen us and be of some practical use in later life. I retained my earlier fondness for stilt walking, and now I was able to devote some time to it. We started with stilts which lifted our feet our own height above ground. As we became more adept we used longer stilts, usually about ten feet high. On those we strutted about the courtyards, peering into windows and generally making a nuisance of ourselves. No balancing pole was used; when we desired to stay in one place we rocked from foot to foot as if we were marking time. That enabled us to maintain our balance and position. There was no risk of falling off if one was reasonably alert. We fought battles on stilts. Two teams of us, usually ten a side, would line up about thirty yards apart, and then on a given signal we would charge each other, uttering wild whoops calculated to frighten off the sky demons. As I have said, I was in a class of boys much older and bigger than myself. This gave me an advantage when it came to stilt fights. The others lumbered along heavily, and I could nip in among them and pull a stilt here and push one there and so send the riders toppling. On horseback I was not so good, but when I had to stand or fall on my own resources, I could make my way.

Another use for stilts, for us boys, was when we crossed streams. We could wade carefully across and save a long detour to the nearest ford. I remember once I was ambling along on six-foot stilts. A stream was in the way and I wanted to cross. The water was deep right from the banks, there was no shallow part at all. I sat on the bank and lowered my stilted legs in. The water came to my knees, as I walked out in midstream it rose to nearly my waist. Just then I heard running footsteps. A man hurried along the path and gave the merest glance at the small boy crossing the water. Apparently, seeing that the stream did not reach my waist, he thought: "Ah! Here is a shallow spot." There was a sudden splash, and the man disappeared completely. Then there was a flurry of water, and the man's head came above the surface, his clutching hands reached the bank, and he hauled himself to the land. His language was truly horrible, and the threats of what he was going to do to me almost curdled my blood. I hurried off to the far bank and when I, too, reached shore, I think that never before had I travelled so fast on stilts.

One danger of stilts was the wind which always seems to be blowing in Tibet. We would be playing in a courtyard, on stilts, and in the excitement of the game we would forget the wind and stride out beyond the sheltering wall. A gust of wind would billow out our robes and over we would go, a tangle of arms, legs and stilts. There were very few casualties. Our studies in judo taught us how to fall without harming ourselves. Often we would have bruises and scraped knees, but we ignored those trifles. Of course there were some who could almost trip over their shadow, some clumsy boys never learn breakfalls and they at times sustained a broken leg or arm.

There was one boy who would walk along on his stilts and then turn a somersault between the shafts. He seemed to hold on the end of the stilts, take his feet from the steps, and twist himself round in a complete circle. Up his feet would go, straight over his head, and down to find the steps every time. He did it time after time, almost never missing a step, or breaking the rhythm of his walk. I could jump on stilts, but the first time I did so I landed heavily, the two steps sheared right off and I made a hasty descent. After that I made sure that the stilt steps were well fastened.

Just before my eighth birthday, the Lama Mingyar Dondup told me that the astrologers had predicted that the day following my birthday would be a good time to "open the Third Eye". This did not upset me at all, I knew that he would be there, and I had complete trust in him. As he had so often told me, with the Third Eye open, I should be able to see people as they were. To us the body was a mere shell activated by the greater self, the Overself that takes over when one is asleep, or leaves this life. We believe that Man is placed in the infirm physical body so that he can learn lessons and progress. During sleep Man returns to a different plane of existence. He lays down to rest, and the spirit disengages itself from the physical body and floats off when sleep comes. The spirit is kept in contact with the physical body by a "silver cord" which is there until the moment of death. The dreams which one has are experiences undergone in the spirit plane of sleep. When the spirit returns to the body, the shock of awaking distorts the dream memory, unless one has had special training, and so the "dream" may appear wildly improbable to one in the waking state. But this will be mentioned rather more fully later when I state my own experiences in this connection.

The aura which surrounds the body, and which anyone can be taught to see under suitable conditions, is merely a reflection of the Life Force burning within. We believe that this force is electric, the same as lightning. Now, in the West, scientists can measure and record the "electric brain waves". People who scoff at such things should remember this and remember, too, the corona of the sun. Here flames protrude millions of miles from the sun's disc. The average person cannot see this corona, but in times of total eclipse it is visible to anyone who cares to look. It really does not matter whether people believe it or not. Disbelief will not extinguish the sun's corona. It is still there. So is the human aura. It was this aura, among other things, which I was going to be able to see when the Third Eye was opened.

CHAPTER SEVEN

THE OPENING OF THE THIRD EYE

My birthday came, and during that day I was at liberty, free from lessons, free from services. The Lama Mingyar Dondup said, in the early morning, "Have an amusing day, Lobsang, we are coming to see you at dusk." It was very pleasant lying on my back, lazing, in the sunlight. Slightly below me I could see the Potala with its roofs agleam. Behind me the blue waters of the Norbu Linga, or Jewel Park, made me wish that I could take a skin boat and drift along. South, I could watch a group of traders crossing the Kyi Chu ferry. The day passed too quickly!

With the death of the day the evening was born, and I went to the little room where I was to stay. There came the murmur of soft felt boots on the stone floor outside, and into the room came three lamas of high degree. They put a herbal compress to my head and bound it tightly in place. In the evening the three came again, and one was the Lama Mingyar Dondup. Carefully the compress was removed, and my forehead wiped clean and dry. A strong-looking lama sat behind me and took my head between his knees. The second lama opened a box and removed an instrument made of shining steel. It resembled a bradawl except that instead of having a round shaft this one was "U"-shaped, and in place of a point there were little teeth around the edge of the "U". For some moments the lama looked at the instrument, and then passed it through the flame of a lamp to sterilize it. The Lama Mingyar Dondup took my hands and said, "This is quite painful, Lobsang, and it can only be done while you are fully conscious. It will not take very long, so try to keep as still as you can." I could see various instruments laid out, and a collection of herbal lotions, and I thought to myself: "Well, Lobsang, my boy, they will finish you one way or the other and there is nothing you can do about it—except keep quiet!"

The lama with the instrument looked round to the others, and said: "All ready? Let us start now, the sun has just set." He pressed the instrument to the centre of my forehead and rotated the handle. For a moment there was a sensation as if someone was pricking me with thorns. To me it seemed that time stood still. There was no particular pain as it penetrated the skin and flesh, but there was a little jolt as the end hit the bone. He applied more pressure, rocking the instrument slightly so that the little teeth would fret through the frontal bone. The pain was not sharp at all, just a pressure and a dull ache. I did not move with the Lama Mingyar Dondup looking on; I would rather have died than make a move or outcry. He had faith in me, as I in him, and I knew that what he did or said was right. He was watching most closely, with a little pucker of muscles in tension at the corners of his mouth. Suddenly there was a little "scrunch" and the instrument penetrated the bone. Instantly its motion was arrested by the very alert operator. He held the handle of the instrument firmly while the Lama Mingyar Dondup passed him a very hard, very clean sliver of wood which had been treated by fire and herbs to make it as hard as steel. This sliver was inserted in the "U" of the instrument and slid down so that it just entered the hole in my head. The lama operating moved slightly to one side so that the Lama Mingyar Dondup could also stand in front of me. Then, at a nod from the latter, the operator, with infinite caution, slid the sliver farther and farther. Suddenly I felt a stinging, tickling sensation apparently in the bridge of my nose. It subsided, and I became aware of subtle scents which I could not identify. That, too, passed away and was replaced by a feeling as if I was pushing, or being pushed, against a resilient veil. Suddenly there was a blinding flash, and at that instant the Lama Mingyar Dondup said *"Stop!"* For a moment the pain was intense, like a searing white flame. It diminished, died and was replace by spirals of colour, and globules of incandescent smoke. The metal instrument was carefully removed. The sliver of wood remained, it would stay in place for two or three weeks and until it was removed I would have to stay in this little room almost in darkness. No one would see me except these three lamas, who would continue my instruction day by day. Until the sliver was removed I would have only the barest necessities to eat and drink. As the projecting sliver was being bound in place so that it could not move, the Lama Mingyar Dondup turned to me and said: "You are now one of us, Lobsang. For the rest of your life you will see people as they are and not as they pretend to be." It was a very strange experience to see these men apparently enveloped in golden flame. Not until later did I realize

76

that their auras were golden because of the pure life they led, and that most people would look very different indeed.

As my new-found sense developed under the skilful ministrations of the lamas I was able to observe that there were other emanations extending beyond the innermost aura. In time I was able to determine the state of a person's health by the colour and intensity of the aura. I was also able to know when they were speaking the truth, or otherwise, by the way the colours fluctuated. But it was not only the human body which was the subject of my clairvoyance. I was given a crystal, which I still have, and in its use I had much practice. There is nothing at all magical in gazing-crystals. They are merely instruments. Just as a microscope, or telescope, can bring normally invisible objects into view by using natural laws, so can a gazing-crystal. It merely serves as a focus for the Third Eye, with which one can penetrate any person's subconscious and retain the memory of facts gleaned. The crystal must be suited to the individual user. Some persons work best with a rock crystal, others prefer a ball of glass. Yet others use a bowl of water or a pure black disc. No matter what they use, the principles involved are the same.

For the first week the room was kept in almost complete darkness. The following week just a glimmer of light was admitted, the amount increasing as the end of the week drew close. On the seventeenth day the room was in full light, and the three lamas came together to remove the sliver. It was very simple. The night before my forehead had been painted with a herbal lotion. In the morning the lamas came and, as before, one took my head between his knees. The operator took hold of the projecting end of the wood with an instrument. There was a sudden sharp jerk—and that is all there was to it. The sliver was out. The Lama Mingyar Dondup put a pad of herbs over the very small spot left, and showed me the sliver of wood. It had turned as black as ebony while in my head. The operator lama turned to a little brazier and placed the wood upon it together with some incense of various kinds. As the combined smoke wafted to the ceiling, so was the first stage of my initiation completed. That night I fell asleep with my head in a whirl; what would Tzu look like now that I saw differently? Father, mother, how would they appear? But there was no answer to such questions yet.

In the morning the lamas came again and examined me carefully. They said that I could now go out with the others, but told me that half my time would be spent with the Lama Mingyar Dondup, who would teach me by intensive methods. The other half of my time would be spent attending classes and services, not so much for the educational side, but to give me a balanced outlook by mixing. A little later I would be taught by hypnotic methods as well. For the moment I was mainly interested in food. For the past eighteen days I had been kept on a very small allowance, now I intended to make up for it. Out of the door I hurried, intent only on that thought. Approaching me was a figure smothered in blue smoke, shot through with flecks of angry red. I uttered a squeak of alarm and dashed back into the room. The others looked up at my horrified expression. "There's a man on fire in the corridor," I said. The Lama Mingyar Dondup hurried out and came back smiling. "Lobsang, that is a cleaner in a temper. His aura is smoky-blue as he is not evolved, and the flecks of red are the temper impulses showing. Now you can again go in search of that food you want so much."

It was fascinating meeting the boys I knew so well, yet had not known at all. Now I could look at them and get the impression of their true thoughts, the genuine liking for me, the jealousy from some, and the indifference from others. It was not just a matter of seeing colours and knowing all; I had to be trained to understand what those colours meant. My Guide and I sat in a secluded alcove where we could watch those who entered the main gates. The Lama Mingyar Dondup would say: "The one coming, Lobsang, do you see that thread of colour vibrating above his heart? That shade and vibration indicates that he has a pulmonary disease", or, perhaps at an approaching trader: "Look at this one, look at those shifting bands, those intermittent flecks. Our Brother of Business is thinking that he may be able to delude the stupid monks, Lobsang, he is remembering that he did so once before. To what petty meannesses men will stoop for money!" As an aged monk approached, the Lama said: "Watch this one carefully, Lobsang. Here is a truly holy man, but one who believes in the literal word-for-word accuracy of our Scriptures. You observe those discolorations in the yellow of the nimbus? It indicates that he has not yet evolved far enough to reason for himself." So it went on, day after day. Particularly with the sick we used the power of the Third Eye, for those who were sick in the flesh or sick in the spirit. One evening the Lama said: "Later we shall show you how to shut the Third Eye at will, for you will not want to watch people's failings all the time, it would be an intolerable burden. For the moment use it all the time, as you do your physical eyes. Then we will train you to shut it and open it at will as you can the other eyes."

Many years ago, according to our legends, all men and women could use the Third Eye. In those days the gods walked upon the earth and mixed with men. Mankind had visions of replacing the gods and tried to kill them, forgetting that what Man could see the gods could see better. As a punishment, the Third Eye of Man was closed. Throughout the ages a few people have been born with the ability to see clairvoyantly; those who have it naturally can have its power increased a thousandfold by appropriate treatment, as I had. As a special talent it had to be treated with care and respect. The Lord Abbot sent for me one day and said: "My son, you now have this ability, an ability denied to most. Use if only for good, never for self-gain. As you wander in other countries you will meet those who would have you behave as a conjurer in a fair. 'Prove us this, prove us that', they will say. But I say, my son, that this must not be. The talent is to enable you to help others, not to enrich self. Whatever you see by clairvoyance—and you will see much!—do not disclose it if it will harm others or affect their Path through Life. For Man must choose his own Path, my son, tell him what you will, he will still go his own way. Help in sickness, in suffering, yes, but do not say that which may alter a man's Path." The Lord Abbot was a very learned man and was the physician who attended the Dalai Lama. Before concluding that interview he told me that within a few days I was going to be sent for by the Dalai Lama who wanted to see me. I was going to be a visitor at the Potala for a few weeks with the Lama Mingyar Dondup.

CHAPTER EIGHT

THE POTALA

ONE Monday morning the Lama Mingyar Dondup told me that
the date for our visit to the Potala had been fixed. It was to be at the
end of the week. "We must rehearse, Lobsang, we must make
ourselves quite perfect in our approach." I was going to be presented to the Dalai Lama, and my "approach" had to be exactly
right. In a little disused temple near our schoolroom there was a
life-sized statue of the Dalai Lama. We went there and pretended
that we were in audience at the Potala. "You see how I do it first,
Lobsang. Enter the room like this, with your eyes down. Walk to
here, about five feet from the Dalai Lama. Put out your tongue in
salute and sink to your knees. Now watch carefully; put your arms
like this and bow forward. Once, once more, and then a third time.
Kneel, with your head bowed, then place the silk scarf across His
feet, like this. Regain your position, with head bowed, so that He
can put a scarf across your neck. Count ten to yourself, so as not
to show undue haste, then rise and walk backwards to the nearest
unoccupied cushion." I had followed all that as the Lama demonstrated it with the ease of long practice. He continued: "Just a
warning here, before you start to walk backwards, take a quick,
unobtrusive glance at the position of the nearest cushion. We
don't want you to catch the cushion with your heels and have to
practise a breakfall to save the back of your head. It is quite easy to
trip in the excitement of the moment. Now you show me that you

can do as well as I." I went out of the room, and the Lama clapped his hands as a signal for me to enter. In I hurried, only to be stopped with: "Lobsang! Lobsang! Are you in for a race? Now do it more slowly; time your steps by saying to yourself, Om-ma-ni-pad-me-Hum! Then you will come in as a dignified young priest instead of a galloping racehorse on the Tsang-po plain." Out I went once more, and this time I entered most sedately and made my way to the statue. On my knees I went, with my tongue protruding in Tibetan salute. My three bows must have been models of perfection; I was proud of them. But, goodness me! I'd forgotten the scarf! So out I went once more to start all over again. This time I did it correctly, and placed the ceremonial scarf at the foot of the statue. I walked backwards, and managed to sit in the lotus fashion without tripping.

"Now we come to the next stage. You will have to conceal your wooden drinking-cup in your left sleeve. You will be given tea when you are seated. The cup is held like this, wedged against the sleeve and forearm. If you are reasonably careful it will stay in place. Let us practise with the cup up the sleeve, and remembering the scarf." Every morning of that week we rehearsed so that I could do it automatically. At first the cup *would* fall out and clatter across the floor when I bowed, but I soon mastered the knack of it. On the Friday I had to go before the Lord Abbot and show him that I was proficient. He said that my performance was "a worthy tribute to the training of our Brother Mingyar Dondup".

The next morning, Saturday, we walked down our hill to go across to the Potala. Our Lamasery was a part of the Potala organization although it was on a separate hill close to the main buildings. Ours was known as the Temple of Medicine, and the Medical School. Our Lord Abbot was the sole physician to the Dalai Lama, a position not altogether to be envied, because his job was not to cure an illness but to keep the patient well. Any aches or disorders were thus considered to be due to some failure on the part of the physician. Yet the Lord Abbot could not go and examine the Dalai Lama whenever he wished, but had to wait until he was sent for, when the patient was ill!

But on this Saturday I was not thinking of the worries of the physician, I had enough of my own. At the foot of our hill we turned towards the Potala and made our way through the crowds of avid sightseers and pilgrims. These people had come from all parts of Tibet to see the home of the Inmost One, as we call the Dalai Lama. If they could catch a glimpse of him they would go away feeling more than repaid for the long journeys and hardships. Some of the pilgrims had travelled for months on foot to make this

81

one visit to the Holy of Holies. Here there were farmers, nobles from distant provinces, herdsmen, traders, and the sick who hoped to obtain a cure in Lhasa. All thronged the road and made the six-mile circuit around the foot of the Potala. Some went on hands and knees, others stretched their length on the ground, arose, and stretched again. Yet others, the sick and infirm, hobbled along supported by friends, or with the aid of two sticks. Everywhere there were the vendors. Some were selling hot buttered tea heated over a swinging brazier. Others were selling foods of various kinds. There were charms for sale and amulets "blessed by a Holy Incarnation". Old men were there selling printed horoscopes to the gullible. Farther down the road a group of cheerful men were trying to sell hand prayer-wheels as a souvenir of the Potala. Scribes were there, too: for a certain sum they would write a note certifying that the person paying them had visited Lhasa and all the holy places there. We had no time for any of these, our objective was the Potala.

The private residence of the Dalai Lama was at the very top of the building, for no one may live higher. An immense stone staircase goes all the way up to the top, running outside the buildings. It is more like a street of stairs than a mere staircase. Many of the higher officials ride their horses up to save them from walking. We met many such during our ascent. At one point, high up, the Lama Mingyar Dondup stopped and pointed: "There is your former home, Lobsang, the servants are very active in the courtyard." I looked, and perhaps it would be better to leave unsaid what I felt. Mother was just riding out with her retinue of servants. Tzu was there as well. No, my thoughts at that time must remain mine.

The Potala is a self-contained township on a small mountain. Here are conducted all the ecclesiastical and secular affairs of Tibet. This building, or group of buildings, is the living heart of the country, the focus of all thoughts, of all hopes. Within these walls are treasure-houses containing blocks of gold, sacks and sacks of gems, and curiosities from the earliest ages. The present buildings are only about three hundred and fifty years old, but they are built on the foundations of a former palace. Long before that there was an armoured fort on the top of the mountain. Deep down inside the mountain, for it is of volcanic origin, there is a huge cave, with passages radiating from it, and at the end of one a lake. Only a few, the very privileged few, have been here, or even know about it.

But outside, in the morning sunlight, we were making our way up the steps. Everywhere we heard the clacking of prayer-wheels—

the only form of wheel in Tibet because of the old prediction which says that when wheels come into the country, peace will go out. Eventually we reached the top where the giant guards swung open the gold gate as they saw the Lama Mingyar Dondup, whom they knew well. We went on until we reached the very top of the roof where were the tombs of former Incarnations of the Dalai Lama, and his present private residence. A large curtain of yaks' wool, coloured maroon, covered the entrance. It was pulled aside at our approach and we entered a large hall which was guarded by green porcelain dragons. Many rich tapestries hung from the walls, depicting religious scenes and ancient legends. On low tables there were articles to delight a collector's heart, statuettes of various gods and goddesses of mythology, and cloisonné ornaments. By a curtain doorway, on a shelf, rested the Book of Nobles, and I wished that I could open it and see our name inside, to reassure me, for on this day, in this place, I felt very small and insignificant. At eight years of age I had no illusions left, and I wondered why the Highest in the Land wanted to see me. I knew that it was highly unusual and it was my opinion that there was more hard work behind it all, hard work or hardship.

A lama robed in cherry-red, with a gold stole around his neck, was talking with the Lama Mingyar Dondup. The latter seemed to be very well known indeed here, and everywhere I had been with him. I heard: "His Holiness is interested, and wants a private talk with him, alone." My Guide turned to me and said: "It is time for you to go in, Lobsang. I will show you the door, then enter alone and pretend that it is just practice again, as we have been doing all this week." He put an arm round my shoulders and led me to a door, whispering, "There is no need at all for you to worry—in you go." With a little push at my back to urge me in he stood and watched. I entered the door, and there, at the far end of a long room, was the Inmost One, the Thirteenth Dalai Lama.

He was sitting on a silken cushion of saffron colour. His dress was that of an ordinary lama, but on his head he wore a tall yellow hat which had flaps reaching to his shoulders. He was just putting down a book. Bowing my head I walked across the floor until I was about five feet away, then I sank to my knees and bowed three times. The Lama Mingyar Dondup had passed me the silk scarf just before I entered, now I placed it at the feet of the Inmost One. He bent forward and put his across my wrists instead of, as was usual, around the neck. I felt dismayed now, I had to walk backwards to the nearest cushion, and I had observed that they were all quite a distance away, near the walls. The Dalai Lama spoke for the first time: "Those cushions are too far away for you to walk backwards, turn around and bring one here so that we can talk together." I did so, and returned with a cushion. He said, "Put it here, in front of me, and sit down." When I was seated, he said, "Now, young man, I have heard some remarkable things about you. You are clairvoyant in your own right, and you have had the power further increased by the Opening of the Third Eye. I have the records of your last incarnation. I have also the astrologers' predictions. You will have a hard time at the start, but will attain success in the end. You will go to many foreign countries the world over, countries of which you have not yet heard. You will see death and destruction and cruelty such as you cannot imagine. The way will be long and hard, but success will come as predicted." I did not know why he was telling me all this, I knew it all, every word of it, and had done since I was seven years of age. I knew well that I would learn medicine and surgery in Tibet and then go to China and learn the same subjects all over again. But the Inmost One was still speaking, warning me not to give proof of any unusual powers, not to talk of the ego, or soul, when I was in the western world. "I have been to India and China," he said, "and in those countries one can discuss the Greater Realities, but I have met many from the West. Their values are not as ours, they worship commerce and gold. Their scientists say: 'Show us the soul. Produce it, let us grasp it, weigh it, test it with acids. Tell us its molecular structure, its chemical reactions. Proof, proof, we must have proof' " they will tell you, uncaring that their negative attitude of suspicion kills any chance of their obtaining that proof. But we must have tea."

He lightly struck a gong, and gave an order to the lama who answered it. Shortly the latter returned bringing tea and special foods which had been imported from India. As we ate the Inmost One talked, telling me of India and China. He told me that he wanted me to study really hard, and that he would pick special teachers for me. I simply could not contain myself; I blurted out: "Oh, no one can know more than my Master, the Lama Mingyar Dondup!" The Dalai Lama looked at me, then put his head back and roared with laughter. Probably no other person had spoken to him like that, certainly no other eight-year-old boy had. He seemed to appreciate it. "So you think Mingyar Dondup is good, do you? Tell me what you really think of him, you young gamecock!" "Sir!" I replied, "you have told me that I have exceptional powers of clairvoyance. The Lama Mingyar Dondup is the best person I have ever seen." The Dalai Lama laughed again and struck the gong at his side. "Ask Mingyar to come in," he said to the lama who answered his summons.

The Lama Mingyar Dondup entered, and made his bows to the Inmost One. "Bring a cushion and sit down, Mingyar," said the Dalai Lama. "You have had your character told by this young man of yours; it is an assessment with which I entirely agree." The Lama Mingyar Dondup sat down beside me, and the Dalai Lama continued, "You have accepted full responsibility for Lobsang Rampa's training. Plan it as you will, and call upon me for any letters of authority. I will see him from time to time." Turning to me, he said, "Young man, you have chosen well, your Guide is an old friend of my former days, and is a true Master of the Occult." There were a few more words, and then we rose, bowed, and left the room. I could see that the Lama Mingyar Dondup was secretly very pleased with me, or with the impression I had made. "We will stay here a few days and explore some of the lesser-known parts of the buildings," he said. "Some of the lower corridors and rooms have not been opened during the past two hundred years. You will learn much Tibetan history from these rooms."

One of the attendant lamas—there were none below that rank in the Dalai Lama's residence—approached and said that we should have a room each here at the top of the building. He showed us to the rooms, and I was quite thrilled at the view, right across Lhasa, right across the plain. The lama said, "His Holiness has given instruction that you come and go as you please and that no door be closed against you."

The Lama Mingyar Dondup told me that I should lie down for a time. The scar on my left leg was still causing much trouble. It was painful, and I walked with a limp. At one time it was feared that I would be a permanent cripple. For an hour I rested, then my Guide came in bearing tea and food. "Time to fill out some of those hollows, Lobsang. They eat well in this place, so let us make the most of it." I needed no further encouragement to eat. When we had finished, the Lama Mingyar Dondup led the way out of the room, and we went into another room at the far side of the flat roof. Here, to my profound amazement, the windows had no oiled cloth, but were filled with nothingness which was just visible. I put out my hand and very cautiously touched the visible nothingness. To my astonishment it was cold, as cold as ice almost, and slippery. Then it dawned upon me: glass! I had never seen the stuff in a sheet before. We had used powdered glass on our kite strings, but that glass had been thick and one could not see clearly through it. It had been coloured, but this, this was like water.

But that was not all. The Lama Mingyar Dondup swung open the window, and picked up a brass tube which seemed to be part of a trumpet covered in leather. He took the tube and pulled, and four pieces appeared, each from inside the other. He laughed at the expression on my face, and then poked one end of the tube out of the window and brought the other end close to his face. Ah! I thought, he is going to play an instrument. But the end did not go to his mouth, but to one eye. He fiddled about with the tube, and then said: "Look through here, Lobsang. Look with your right eye and keep the left closed." I looked, and nearly fainted with stupefaction. A man on a horse was riding up the tube towards me. I jumped aside, and looked around. There was no one in the room except the Lama Mingyar Dondup, and he was shaking with laughter. I looked at him suspiciously, thinking that he had bewitched me. "His Holiness said you were a Master of the Occult," I said, "but do you have to make fun of your pupil?" He laughed all the more, and motioned for me to look again. With considerable misgivings I did so, and my Guide moved the tube slightly so that I saw a different view. A telescope! Never before had I seen one. Never have I forgotten that sight of a man on a horse riding up inside the tube towards me. I am often reminded of it when a western person says "Impossible!" to some statement about the occult. That was certainly "impossible" to me. The Dalai Lama had brought a number of telescopes with him when he returned from India, and he was very fond of looking over the surrounding countryside. Here, too, I looked into a mirror for the first time and I certainly did not recognize the horrible looking creature that I saw. I saw a pale-faced little boy who had a large red scar in the middle of his forehead, and a nose which was undeniably prominent. I had seen my faint reflection before in water, but this was too plain. I have not bothered with mirrors since.

It may be thought that Tibet was a peculiar country to be without glass, telescopes or mirrors, but people did not want such things. Nor did we want wheels. Wheels made for speed, and for so-called civilization. We have long realized that in the rush of commercial life there is no time for the things of the mind. Our physical world had proceeded at a leisurely pace, so that our esoteric knowledge could grow, and expand. We have for thousands of years known the truth of clairvoyance, telepathy, and other branches of metaphysics. While it is quite true that many lamas can sit naked in the snow, and by thought alone melt the snow around them, such things are not demonstrated for the delight of the mere sensation seeker. Some lamas, who are masters of the occult, definitely can levitate, but they do not display their powers to entertain naïve onlookers. The teacher, in Tibet, always makes sure that his pupil is morally fit to be trusted with such powers. It follows from this, that as the teacher must be absolutely sure of the moral integrity of the student, metaphysical powers are never abused, as only the right people are taught. Those powers are in no way magical, they are merely the outcome of using natural laws.

In Tibet there are some who can best develop in company, and others who have to retire to solitude. These latter men go to outlying lamaseries and enter a hermit's cell. It is a small room, usually built on the side of a mountain. The stone walls are thick, perhaps six feet thick so that no sound can penetrate. The hermit enters, at his own desire, and the entrance is walled up. There is no light whatever, no furnishings, nothing but the empty stone box. Food is passed in once a day through a light-trapped, sound-proofed hatch. Here the hermit stays, first for three years, three months and three days. He meditates on the nature of Life, and on the nature of Man. For no reason whatever can he leave that cell in the physical body. During the last month of his stay a very small hole is made in the roof to allow a faint ray of light to enter. It is enlarged day by day so that the hermit's eyes become used to the light once again. Otherwise he would go blind as soon as he emerged. Very often these men return to their cell after only a few weeks, and stay there for life. It is not such a sterile, worthless existence as one might suppose. Man is a spirit, a creature of another world, and once he can become free of the bonds of the flesh, he can roam the world as a spirit and can help by thought. Thoughts, as we in Tibet well know, are waves of energy. Matter is energy condensed. It is thought, carefully directed and partly condensed, which can cause an object to move "by thought". Thought, controlled in another way, can result in telepathy, and can cause a person at a distance to do a certain action. Is this so very difficult to believe, in a world which regards as commonplace the act of a man speaking into a microphone guiding a plane to land in dense fog, when the pilot can see no ground at all? With a little training, and no scepticism, Man could do this by telepathy instead of making use of a fallible machine.

My own esoteric development did not entail this prolonged seclusion in total darkness. It took another form which is not available to the larger number of men who want to become hermits. My training was directed towards a specific purpose, and by direct order of the Dalai Lama. I was taught such things by another method, as well as by hypnosis, which cannot be discussed in a book of this nature. It will suffice to state that I was given more enlightenment than the average hermit can obtain in a very long lifetime. My visit to the Potala was in connection with the first stages of this training, but more of that later.

I was fascinated by that telescope, and I used it quite a lot to examine the places I knew so well. The Lama Mingyar Dondup explained the principles in minute detail so that I could understand that there was no magic involved, but just ordinary laws of nature.

Everything was explained, not merely about the telescope, but reasons were given as to why a certain thing happened. I could never say "Oh! it is magic!" without having an explanation of the laws involved. Once during this visit I was taken to a perfectly dark room. The Lama Mingyar Dondup said, "Now you stand here, Lobsang, and watch that white wall." Then he blew out the flame of the butter-lamp and did something to the shutter of the window. Instantly there appeared on the wall before me a picture of Lhasa, but upside down! I shouted with amazement at the sight of men, women, and yaks walking about upside down. The picture suddenly flickered, and everything was the right way up. The explanation about "bending light rays" really puzzled me more than anything; how *could* one bend light? I had had demonstrated to me the method of breaking jars and pitchers with a soundless whistle, that was quite simple and not worth a further thought, but *bending light*! Not until a special piece of apparatus, consisting of a lamp the light of which was hidden by various slats, was brought from another room, could I understand the matter. Then I could see the rays bend, and nothing surprised me after.

The storerooms of the Potala were crammed full of wonderful statues, ancient books, and most beautiful wall paintings of religious subjects. The very, very few western people who have seen any of them, consider them to be indecent. They portray a male and a female spirit in close embrace, but the intention of these pictures is very far from being obscene, and no Tibetan would ever regard them as such. These two nude figures in embrace are meant to convey the ecstasy which follows the union of Knowledge and Right Living. I admit that I was horrified beyond measure when I first saw that the Christians worshipped a tortured man nailed to a cross as their symbol. It is such a pity that we all tend to judge the peoples of other countries by our own standards.

For centuries gifts have been arriving at the Potala from various countries, gifts for the Dalai Lama of the time. Nearly all these presents have been stored in rooms, and I had a wonderful time turning out and obtaining psychometrical impressions as to why the things were sent in the first place. It was indeed an education in motives. Then, after I had stated my impression as obtained from the object, my Guide would read from a book and tell me the exact history, and what had happened after. I was pleased at his more and more frequent, "You are quite right, Lobsang, you are doing very well indeed."

Before leaving the Potala we made a visit to one of the underground tunnels. I was told that I could visit just one, as I would see the others at a later date. We took flaring torches and cautiously climbed down what seemed to be endless steps, and slithered along smooth rocky passages. These tunnels, I was told, had been made by volcanic action countless centuries before. On the walls were strange diagrams and drawings of quite unfamiliar scenes. I was more interested in seeing the lake which I had been told stretched for miles and miles at the end of one passage. At last we entered a tunnel which grew wider and wider, until suddenly the roof disappeared to where the light of our torches would not reach. A hundred yards more, and we stood at the edge of water such as I had never seen before. It was black and still, with the blackness that made it appear almost invisible, more like a bottomless pit than a lake. Not a ripple disturbed the surface, not a sound broke the silence. The rock upon which we stood also was black, it glistened in the light of the torches, but a little to one side was a glitter on the wall. I walked towards it, and saw that in the rock there was a broad band of gold that was perhaps fifteen to twenty feet long and reached from my neck to my knees. Great heat had once started to melt it from the rock, and it had cooled in lumps like golden candle grease. The Lama Mingyar Dondup broke the silence: "This lake goes to the River Tsang-po forty miles away. Years and years ago an adventurous party of monks made a raft of wood, and made paddles with which to propel it. They stocked the raft with torches, and pushed off from the shore. For miles they paddled, exploring, then they came to an even larger space where they could not see walls or roof. They drifted on as they paddled gently, not sure which way to go."

I listened, picturing it vividly. The Lama continued: "They were lost, not knowing which was forward or which was backward. Suddenly the raft lurched, there was a blast of wind which extinguished their torches, leaving them in complete darkness, and they felt that their fragile craft was in the grip of the Water Demons. Around they spun, leaving them giddy and sick. They clung to the ropes that held the wood together. With the violent motion, little waves washed over the top and they became wet through. Their speed increased, they felt that they were in the grip of a ruthless giant pulling them to their doom. How long they travelled they had no means of telling. There was no light, the darkness was solid black, such as never was upon the surface of the earth. There was a scraping, grating noise, and stunning blows and crushing pressures. They were flung off the raft and forced under the water. Some of them had just time to gulp air. Others were not so fortunate. Light appeared, greenish and uncertain, it became brighter. They were twisted and thrown, then they shot up into brilliant sunshine.

Two of them managed to reach the shore more than half drowned, battered and bleeding. Of the other three there was no trace. For hours they lay half between death and life. Eventually one roused sufficiently to look about him. He nearly collapsed again from the shock. In the distance was the Potala. Around them were green meadows with grazing yaks. At first they thought that they had died, and this was a Tibetan Heaven. Then they heard footsteps beside them, and a herdsman was looking down at them. He had seen the floating wreckage of the raft and had come to collect it for his own use. Eventually the two monks managed to convince the man that they were monks, for their robes had been completely torn off, and he agreed to go to the Potala for litters. Since that day very little has been done to explore the lake, but it is known that there are islands a little way beyond the range of our torches. One of them has been explored, and what was found you will see later when you are initiated.

I thought of it all and wished that I could have a raft and explore the lake. My Guide had been watching my expression: suddenly he laughed and said: "Yes, it *would* be fun to explore, but why waste our bodies when we can do the search in the astral! You can, Lobsang. Within a very few years you will be competent to explore this place with me, and add to the total knowledge we have of it. But for now, study, boy, study. For both of us."

Our torches were flickering low and it seemed to me that we should soon be groping blindly in the darkness of the tunnels. As we turned away from the lake I thought how foolish of us not to bring spare lights. At that moment the Lama Mingyar Dondup turned to the far wall and felt about. From some hidden niche he produced more torches and lit them from those now almost smouldering out.

"We keep spares here, Lobsang, because it would be difficult to find one's way out in the dark. Now let us be going."

Up the sloping passages we toiled, pausing a while to regain our breath and to look at some of the drawings on the walls. I could not understand them, they appeared to be of giants, and there were machines so strange as to be utterly beyond my comprehension. Looking at my Guide I could see that he was quite at home with these drawings, and in the tunnels. I was looking forward to other visits here, there was some mystery about it all, and

I never could hear of a mystery without trying to get to the bottom of it. I could not bear the idea of spending years guessing at a solution when there was a chance of finding the answer, even if in so doing I was involved in considerable danger. My thoughts were interrupted by: "Lobsang! Your are mumbling like an old man. We have a few more steps to go, and then it is daylight again. We will go on the roof and use the telescope to point out the site where those monks of old came to the surface."

When we did so, when we were on the roof, I wondered why we could not ride the forty miles and actually visit the place. The Lama Mingyar Dondup told me that there was nothing much to see, certainly nothing that the telescope would not reveal. The outlet from the lake was apparently far below the water-level and there was nothing to mark the spot, except a clump of trees which had been planted there by order of the previous Incarnation of the Dalai Lama.

CHAPTER NINE

AT THE WILD ROSE FENCE

THE next morning we made our leisurely preparations to return to Chakpori. For us the Potala visit was quite a holiday. Before leaving I rushed up to the roof to have a last look at the countryside through the telescope. On a roof of the Chakpori a small acolyte was lying on his back reading, and occasionally tossing small pebbles on to the bald heads of monks in the courtyard. Through the glass I could see the impish grin on his face as he ducked back out of sight of the puzzled monks below. It made me acutely uncomfortable to realize that the Dalai Lama had no doubt watched me do similar tricks. In future, I resolved, I would confine my efforts to the side of the buildings hidden from the Potala.

But it was time to leave. Time to say our thanks to those lamas who had worked to make our short stay so pleasant. Time to be particularly nice to the Dalai Lama's personal steward. He had charge of the "foods from India". I must have pleased him, because he made me a farewell gift which I was not slow to eat. Then, fortified, we started down the steps on our way back to the Iron Mountain. As we reached halfway we became aware of shouts and calls, and passing monks pointed back, behind us. We stopped, and a breathless monk rushed down and gasped out a message to the Lama Mingyar Dondup. My Guide halted.

"Wait here for me, Lobsang, I shall not be very long." With that he turned and walked up the steps again. I idled around, admiring the view, and looking at my former home. Thinking of it, I turned, and almost fell over backwards as I saw my father riding towards me. As I looked at him he looked at me and his lower jaw dropped slightly as he recognized me. Then, to my unutterable pain, he ignored me, and rode on. I looked at his retreating back and called "Father!" He took no notice whatever, but rode stolidly on. My eyes felt hot, I began to tremble, and I thought that I was going to disgrace myself in public, on the steps of the Potala of all places. With more self-control than I thought I possessed I straightened my back and gazed out over Lhasa.

After about half an hour the Lama Mingyar Dondup came riding down the steps and leading another horse.

"Get on, Lobsang, we have to get to Sera in a hurry, one of the abbots there has had a bad accident."

I saw that there was a case tied to each saddle, and guessed that it was my Guide's equipment. Along the Lingkhor road we galloped, past my former home, scattering pilgrims and beggars alike. It did not take us long to reach Sera Lamasery, where monks were waiting for us. We jumped off the horses, each carrying a case, and an abbot led us in to where an old man lay on his back.

His face was the colour of lead, and the life force seemed to be flickering almost to a halt. The Lama Mingyar Dondup called for boiling water, which was ready, and into it he dropped certain herbs. While I was stirring this, the Lama examined the old man, who had a fractured skull as a result of falling. A piece of bone was depressed and was exerting pressure on the brain. When the liquid was cool enough we mopped the old man's head with it, and my Guide cleaned his hands with some of it. Taking a sharp knife from his case, he quickly made a U-shaped cut through the flesh, right through to the bone. There was little bleeding, the herbs prevented it. More herbal lotion was mopped on, and the flap of flesh was turned back and cleared away from the bone. Very, very gently the Lama Mingyar Dondup examined the area and found where the skull bone had been crushed in and was hanging below the normal level of the skull. He had put a lot of instruments into a bowl of disinfecting lotion before commencing, now he took from the bowl two silver rods, flattened at one end, and with serrations in the flat part. With extreme care he inserted the thinnest edge into the widest fracture of the bone and held it rigidly while he took a firmer grip of the bone with the other rod. Gently, very gently, he prised up the flap of bone so that it was just above the normal level. He wedged it there with one rod and said: "Now pass the bowl, Lobsang." I held it so that he could take what he wanted, and he took a small spike of silver, just a minute triangular wedge. This he pressed into the crack between the normal skull bone and the fractured edge, which was now slightly above the level. Slowly he pressed the bone a little. It moved slightly, and he pressed just a little more. The level was now normal. "It will knit together, and the silver, being an inert metal, will cause no trouble." He mopped the area with more herbal lotion, and carefully put back the flap of flesh which had been left attached by one side. With boiled hair from a horse's tail he stitched the flap, and covered the site of the operation with a herbal paste tied in place with boiled cloth.

The old abbot's life force had been growing stronger since the pressure was relieved from his brain. We propped him up with cushions so that he was in a semi-sitting position. I cleaned the instruments in fresh boiling lotion, dried them on boiled cloth and packed everything carefully back into the two cases. As I was cleaning my hands after, the old man's eyes flickered open, and he gave a weak smile as he saw the Lama Mingyar Dondup bending over him.

"I knew that only you could save me, that is why I sent the mind message to the Peak. My task is not yet finished and I am not ready to leave the body."

My Guide looked at him carefully and replied: "You will recover from this. A few days of discomfort, a headache or two, and when that has gone you can go about your work. For a few days you must have someone with you when you sleep, so that you do not lie flat. After three or four days you will have no cause for worry."

I had gone to the window and was looking out. It was quite interesting to see conditions in another lamasery. The Lama Mingyar Dondup came to me and said: "You did well, then, Lobsang, we shall make a team. Now I want to show you around this community, it is very different from ours."

We left the old abbot in the care of a lama, and went out into the corridor. The place was not so clean as at Chakpori, nor did there seem to be any strict discipline. Monks seemed to come and go as they pleased. The temples were uncared for, compared to ours, and even the incense was more bitter. Gangs of boys were playing in the courtyards—at Chakpori they would have been hard at work. The prayer-wheels were for the most part unturned. Here and there an aged monk sat and twirled the Wheels, but there was none of the order, cleanliness, and discipline which I had come to take as average. My Guide said: "Well, Lobsang, would you like to stay here and have their easy life?"

"No, I would not, I think they are a lot of savages here," I said.

He laughed. "Seven thousand of them! It is always the noisy few who bring the silent majority into disrepute."

"That may be," I replied. "but although they call this the Rose Fence, that is not what I would call it."

He looked at me with a smile: "I believe you would take on the job of bringing discipline to this lot single-handed."

It was a fact that our Lamasery had the strictest discipline of any, most of the others were very lax indeed, and when the monks there wanted to laze, well, they just lazed and nothing was said about it. Sera, or the Wild Rose Fence as it is really called, is three miles from the Potala and is one of the lamaseries known as "The Three Seats". Drebung is the largest of the three, with not less than ten thousand monks. Sera comes next in importance with about seven thousand five hundred monks, while Ganden is the least important with a mere six thousand. Each is like a complete town with streets, colleges, temples, and all the usual buildings that go to make up a township. The streets were patrolled by the Men of Kham. Now, no doubt, they are patrolled by Communist soldiers! Chakpori was a small community, but an important one. As the Temple of Medicine, it was then the "Seat of Medical Learning" and was well represented in the Council Chamber of the government.

At Chakpori we were taught what I shall term "judo". That is the nearest English word I can find, the Tibetan description of *sung-thru- kyöm-pa tü de-po le-la-po* cannot be translated, nor can our "technical" word of *amarëe*. "Judo" is a very elementary form of our system. Not all lamaseries have this training, but we at Chakpori were taught it to give us self-control, to enable us to deprive others of consciousness for medical purposes, and to enable us to travel safely in rougher parts of the country. As medical lamas we travelled extensively.

Old Tzu had been a teacher of the art, perhaps the best exponent of it in Tibet, and he had taught me all he knew—for his own satisfaction in doing a job well. Most men and boys knew the elementary holds and throws, but I knew them when I was four years of age. This art, we believe, should be used for self-defence and self-control, and not after the manner of a prize-fighter. We are of the opinion that the strong man can afford to be gentle, while the weak and unsure brag and boast.

Our judo was used to deprive a person of consciousness when, for instance, setting broken bones, or extracting teeth. There is no pain with it, and no risk. A person can be made unconscious before he is aware of its onset, and he can be restored to full consciousness hours or seconds later without ill effect. Curiously enough, a person made unconscious while speaking will complete the sentence upon awakening. Because of the obvious dangers of this higher system, this and "instant" hypnotism were taught only to those who could pass most stringent tests of character. And then hypnotic blocks were imposed so that one should not abuse the powers conferred.

In Tibet, a lamasery is not merely a place where men of religious inclination live, but a self-contained town with all the usual facilities and amenities. We had our theatres in which to see religious and traditional plays. Musicians were ever ready to entertain us, and prove that in no other community were there such good players. Those monks who had money were able to buy food, clothing, luxuries, and books in the shops. Those who desired to save, deposited their cash in the lamastic equivalent of a bank. All communities, in any part of the world, have their offenders against the rules. Ours were arrested by monk-police and taken off to a court where they were given a fair trial. If found guilty, they had to serve their sentence in the lamastic prison. Schools of various types catered for all grades of mentality. Bright boys were helped to make their way, but in all lamaseries other then Chakpori, the slothful person was permitted to sleep or dream his life away. Our idea was, one cannot influence the life of another, so let him catch up in his next incarnation. At Chakpori matters were different, and if one did not make progress, one was compelled to leave and seek sanctuary elsewhere where the discipline was not so strict.

Our sick monks were well treated, we had a hospital in the lamaseries and the indisposed were treated by monks who were trained in medicine and elementary surgery. The more severe cases were treated by specialists, such as the Lama Mingyar Dondup. Quiet often since leaving Tibet I have had to laugh at the Western stories about Tibetans thinking that a man's heart is on the left side, and a woman's is on the right. We saw enough dead bodies cut open to *know* the truth. I have also been much amused about the "filthy Tibetans, riddled with V.D.". The writers of such statements apparently have never been in those convenient places, in England and America, where the local citizenry are offered "Free and Confidential Treatment". We *are* filthy; some of our women, for instance, put stuff on the face, and have to mark the position of the lips so that one cannot miss. Most times they put stuff on their hair to make it shine, or to alter the colour. They even pluck eyebrows and colour nails, sure signs that Tibetan women are "filthy and depraved".

But to return to our lamastic community; often there were visitors, they might be traders or monks. They were given accommodation in the lamastic hotel. They also paid for such accommodation! Not all monks were celibate. Some thought that "single blessedness" did not induce the right frame of mind for contemplation. Those were able to join a special sect of Red Hat monks who were permitted to marry. They were in the minority. The Yellow Hats, a celibate sect, were the ruling class in religious life. In "married" lamaseries, monks and nuns worked side by side in a well-ordered community, and most times the "atmosphere" there was not so rough as in a purely male community.

Certain lamaseries had their own printing-works so that they could print their own books. Usually they made their own paper. This latter was not a healthy occupation, because one form of tree bark used in paper manufacture was highly poisonous. While this prevented any insect from attacking Tibetan paper, it also had a bad effect on the monks, and those who worked at this trade complained of severe headaches and worse. In Tibet we did not use metal type. All our pages were drawn on wood of suitable character, and then everything except the drawn outlines was pared away, leaving the parts to be printed standing high above the rest of the board. Some of these boards were three feet wide by eighteen inches deep and the detail would be quite intricate. No board containing the slightest mistake was used. Tibetan pages are not like the pages of this book, which are longer than they are wide: we used wide and short pages, and they were always unbound. The various loose sheets were kept between carved wooden covers. In printing, the carved board of page contents was laid flat. One monk ran an ink roller over the whole surface, making sure of even distribution. Another monk took up a sheet of paper and quickly spread it on the board, while a third monk followed with a heavy roller to press the paper well down. A fourth monk lifted off the printed page and passed it to an apprentice, who put it to one side. There were very few smudged sheets, these were never used for the book, but were kept for the apprentices to practise upon. At Chakpori we had carved wooden boards about six feet high and about four feet wide: these had carvings of the human figure and the various organs. From them were made wall charts, which we had to colour. We had astrological charts as well. The charts on which we erected horoscopes were about two feet square. In effect they were maps of the heavens at the time of a person's conception and birth. On the map-blanks we inserted the data which we found in the carefully prepared mathematical tables which we published.

After looking over the Rose Fence Lamasery and, in my case, comparing it unfavourably with ours, we returned to the room to see the old abbot again. During the two hours of our absence he had improved very greatly and was now able to take much greater interest in things around him. In particular he was able to pay attention to the Lama Mingyar Dondup, to whom he seemed very attached. My Guide said: "We must leave now, but here are some powdered herbs for you. I will give full instructions to your Priest in Charge as we leave." Three little leather bags were taken from his case and handed over. Three little bags which meant life, instead of death, to an aged man.

In the entrance courtyard we found a monk holding two deplorably frisky ponies. They had been fed and rested and were now very ready to gallop. I was not. Fortunately for me, the Lama Mingyar Dondup was quite content for us to amble along. The Rose Fence is about three thousand seven hundred yards from the nearest part of the Lingkhor road. I was not anxious to pass my old home. My Guide evidently caught my thoughts, for he said: "We will cross the road to the Street of Shops. There is no hurry; tomorrow is a new day which we have not yet seen."

I was fascinated to look at the shops of the Chinese traders and to listen to their high shrill voices as they bickered and chaffered at the prices. Just opposite their side of the street was a chorten, symbolizing immortality of the ego, and behind that loomed a gleaming temple to which the monks of nearby Shede Gompa were streaming. A few minutes' ride and we were in the lanes of cluttered houses which clustered as if for protection in the shadow of the Jo-Kank. "*Ah!*" I thought, "last time I was here I was a free man, not training to be a monk. Wish it was all a dream and I could wake up!" Down the road we ambled, and turned right to the road which led over the Turquoise Bridge. The Lama Mingyar Dondup turned to me and said: "So you still do not want to be a monk? It is quite a good life, you know. At the end of this week the annual party are going to the hills to gather herbs. This time I do not want you to go. Instead, study with me so that you can take the examination for Trappa when you are twelve. I have planned to take you on a special expedition to the highlands to obtain some very rare herbs." Just then we had reached the end of the village of Shö and were approaching the Pargo Kaling, the Western Gate of the Valley of Lhasa. A beggar shrunk against the wall: "Ho! Reverend Holy Lama of Medicine, please do not cure me of my ills or my living is gone." My Guide looked sad as we rode through the chorten forming the gate. "So many of these beggars, Lobsang, so unnecessary. It is they who give us a bad name abroad. In India, and in China, where I went with the Precious One, people talked of the beggars of Lhasa, not realizing that some of them were rich. Well, well, perhaps after the fulfilment of the Prophecy of the Year of the Iron Tiger (1950—Communists invade Tibet) the beggars will be put to work. You and I will not be here to see it, Lobsang. For you, foreign lands. For me, a return to the Heavenly Fields."

It made me sad beyond measure to think that my beloved Lama would leave me, leave this life. Not then did I realize that life on Earth was but an illusion, a testing-place, a school. A knowledge of Man's behaviour to those beset by adversity was beyond me. Now it is not!

Left we turned into the Lingkhor road, past the Kundu Ling, and left again to our own road leading up to the Iron Mountain. I never tired of looking at the coloured rock-carving which made up one side of our mountain. The whole cliff face was covered with carvings and paintings of deities. But the day was far advanced and we had no more time to spare. As we rode up I thought of the herb gatherers. Every year a party from the Chakpori went to the hills to gather herbs, dried them, and packed them into airtight bags. Here, in the hills, was one of the great storehouses of Nature's remedies. Very few people indeed had ever been to the highlands where there were things too strange to discuss. Yes, I decided, I could well forgo a visit to the hills this year, and I would study hard so that I should be fit to accompany the expedition to the highlands when the Lama Mingyar Dondup thought fit. The astrologers had said that I would pass the examination at the first attempt, but I knew that I should have to study hard; I knew that the prediction meant *if* I studied hard enough! My mental stage was at least equivalent to an eighteen-year-old, as always I had mixed with people much older than I, and I had to fend for myself.

CHAPTER TEN

TIBETAN BELIEFS

It may be of some interest to give here some details of our way of life. Our religion is a form of Buddhism, but there is no word which can be transliterated. We refer to it as "The Religion", and to those of our faith as "Insiders". Those of other beliefs are termed "Outsiders". The nearest word, already known in the West, is Lamaism. It departs from Buddhism in that ours is a religion of hope and a belief in the future. Buddhism, to us, seems negative, a religion of despair. We certainly do not think that an all-seeing father is watching and guarding everyone, everywhere.

Many learned people have passed erudite comment on our religion. Many of them have condemned us because they were blinded by their own faith, and could see no other point of view. Some have even called us "satanic" because our ways are alien to them. Most of these writers have based their opinions on hearsay or on the writings of others. Possibly a very few have studied our beliefs for a few days and have then felt competent to know all, to write books on the subject, and to interpret and make known that which it takes our cleverest sages a lifetime to discover.

Imagine the teachings of a Buddhist or Hindu who had flipped the pages of the Christian Bible for an hour or two and then tried to explain all the subtler points of Christianity! *None* of these writers on Lamaism has lived as a monk in a lamasery from early boyhood and studied the Sacred Books. These Books are secret; secret because they are not available to those who want quick, effortless and cheap salvation. Those who want the solace of some ritual, some form of self-hypnosis, can have it if it will help them.

It is not the Inner Reality, but childish self-deception. To some it may be very comforting to think that sin after sin can be committed and then, when the conscience prods too much, a gift of some kind to the nearest temple will so overwhelm the gods with gratitude that forgiveness will be immediate, all-embracing, and certain, and will enable one to indulge in a fresh set of sins. There *is* a God, a Supreme Being. What does it matter what we call Him? God is a fact.

Tibetans who have studied the true teachings of Buddha never pray for mercy or for favours, but only that they may receive justice from Man. A Supreme Being, as the essence of justice, cannot show mercy to one and not to another, because to do so would be a denial of justice. To pray for mercy or for favours, promising gold or incense if the prayer is answered, is to imply that salvation is available to the highest bidder, that God is short of money and can be "bought".

Man can show mercy to Man, but very rarely does; the Supreme Being can show only justice. We are immortal souls. Our prayer: "Om! ma-ni pad-me Hum!"—which is written below—is often translated literally as "Hail to the Jewel of the Lotus!" We who have gone a little further know that the true meaning is "Hail to Man's Overself!" There is *no* death. As one doffs one's clothes at the end of day, so does the soul doff the body when the latter sleeps. As a suit of clothes is discarded when worn out, so does the soul discard the body when the latter is worn or torn. Death is Birth. Dying is merely the act of being born in another plane of existence. Man, or the spirit of Man, is eternal. The body is but the temporary garment that clothes the spirit, to be chosen according to the task in hand upon earth. Outward appearance does not matter. The soul within does. A great prophet may come in the guise of a pauper—how better can one judge of Man's charity to Man!—while one who has sinned in a past life when there is not poverty to drive him on.

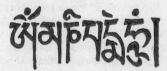

Om! ma-ni pad-me Hum!

"The Wheel of Life" is what we call the act of being born, living on some world, dying, going back to the spirit state, and in time being reborn in different circumstances and conditions. A man may suffer much in a life, it does not necessarily mean that he was evil in a past life; it may be the best and quickest way of learning certain things. Practical experience is a better teacher than hearsay! One who commits suicide may be reborn to live out the years cut short in the past life, but it does not follow that all who die young, or as babies, were suicides. The Wheel of Life applies to all, beggars and kings, men and women, coloured people and white. The Wheel is but a symbol of course, but one which makes matters clear to those who have no time to make a long study of the subject. One cannot explain Tibetan belief in a paragraph or two: the Kangyur, or Tibetan Scriptures, consist of over a hundred books on the subject, and even then it is not fully dealt with. There are many books hidden within remote lamaseries which are seen by Initiates alone.

For centuries peoples of the East have known of the various occult forces and laws and that these were natural. Instead of trying to disprove such forces on the grounds that as they could not be weighed or tested with acids, they could not exist, Eastern scientists and researchers have striven to increase their command over these laws of nature. The mechanics of clairvoyance, for example, did not interest us, the results of clairvoyance did. Some people doubt clairvoyance; they are like the born blind who say that sight is impossible because *they* have not experienced it, because *they* cannot understand how an object some distance away can be seen when there is clearly no contact between it and the eyes!

People have auras, coloured outlines which surround the body, and by the intensity of those colours those experienced in the art can deduce a person's health, integrity, and general state of evolution. The aura is the radiation of the inner life force, the ego, or soul. Around the head is a halo, or nimbus, which also is part of the force. At death the light fades as the ego leaves the body on its journey to the next stage of existence. It becomes a "ghost". It drifts a little, perhaps dazed by the sudden shock of being free of the body. It may not be fully aware of what is happening. That is why lamas attend the dying that they may be informed of the stages through which they will pass. If this is neglected, the spirit may be earthbound by desires of the flesh. It is the duty of the priests to break these ties.

At frequent intervals we had a service for Guiding the Ghosts. Death has no terror for Tibetans, but we believe that one can have an easier passage from this life to the next if certain precautions are taken. It is necessary to follow clearly defined paths, and to think along certain lines. The service would be conducted in a temple with about three hundred monks present. In the centre of the temple would be a group of perhaps five telepathic lamas sitting in a circle, face to face. As the monks, led by an abbot, chanted, the lamas would try to maintain telepathic contact with distressed souls. No translation from the Tibetan Prayers can do full justice to them, but this is an attempt:

"Hear the voices of our souls, all you who wander unguided in the Borderlands. The living and the dead live in worlds apart. Where can their faces be seen and their voices heard? The first stick of incense is lit to summon a wandering ghost that he may be guided.

"Hear the voices of our souls, all you who wander. This is the World of Illusion. Life is but a dream. All that are born must die. Only the Way of Buddha leads to eternal life. The third stick of incense is lit to summon a wandering ghost that he may be guided.

"Hear the voices of our souls all you of great power, you who have been enthroned with mountains and rivers under your rule. Your reigns have lasted but a moment, and the complaints of your peoples have never ceased. The earth runs with blood, and the leaves of the trees are swayed by the sighs of the oppressed. The fourth stick of incense is lit to summon the ghosts of kings and dictators that they may be guided.

"Hear the voices of our souls, all you warriors who have invaded, wounded and killed. Where are your armies now? The earth groans, and weeds grow over the battlefields. The fifth stick of incense is lit to summon lonely ghosts of generals and lords for guidance.

"Hear the voices of our souls, all artists and scholars, you who have worked at painting and writing. In vain you have strained your sight and worn down your ink-slabs. Nothing of you is remembered, and your souls must continue on. The sixth stick of incense is lit to summon the ghosts of artists and scholars for guidance.

"Hear the voices of our souls, beautiful virgins and ladies of high degree whose youth could be compared to a fresh spring morning. After the embrace of lovers comes the breaking of hearts. The autumn, then the winter, comes, trees and flowers fade, as do beauty, and become but skeletons. The seventh stick of incense is lit to summon the wandering ghosts of virgins and ladies of high degree that they may be guided away from the ties of the world.

"Hear the voices of our souls, all beggars and thieves and those who have committed crimes against others and who cannot now obtain rest. You soul wanders friendless in the world, and you have not justice within you. The eighth stick of incense is lit to summon all those ghosts who have sinned and who now wander alone.

"Hear the voices of our souls, prostitutes, women of the night, and all those that have been sinned against and who now wander alone in ghostly realms. The ninth stick of incense is lit to summon them for guidance that they may be freed from the bonds of the world."

In the incense-laden dusk of the temple the flickering butter-lamps would cause living shadows to dance behind the golden images. The air would grow tense with the concentration of the telepathic monks as they strove to maintain contact with those who had passed from the world, yet were still bound to it.

Russet-robed monks sitting in lines facing each other, would intone the Litany of the Dead, and hidden drums would beat out the rhythm of the human heart. From other parts of the temple, as in the living body, would come the growling of internal organs, the rustling of body fluids, and the sighing of air in the lungs. As the ceremony continued, with directions to those who had passed over, the tempo of the body sounds would change, become slow, until at last would come the sounds of the spirit leaving the body. A rustling, quavering gasp, and—silence. The silence that comes with death. Into that silence would come an awareness, discernible to even the least psychic, that other things were around, waiting, listening. Gradually, as the telepathic instruction continued, the tension would lessen as the unquiet spirits moved on towards the next stage of their journey.

We believe, firmly, that we are reborn time after time. But not merely to this earth. There are millions of worlds, and we know that most of them are inhabited. Those inhabitants may be in very different forms to those we know, they may be superior to humans. We in Tibet have never subscribed to the view that Man is the highest and most noble form of evolution. We believe that much higher life forms are to be found elsewhere, and they do not drop atom bombs. In Tibet I have seen records of strange craft in the skies. "The Chariots of the Gods" most people called them. The Lama Mingyar Dondup told me that a group of lamas had established telepathic communication with these "gods", who said that they were watching Earth, apparently in much the same way as humans watch wild and dangerous animals in a zoo.

Much has been written about levitation. It is possible, as I have often seen it, but it takes much practice. There is no real point in engaging in levitation as there is a far simpler system. Astral travelling is easier and surer. Most lamas do it, and anyone who is prepared to use some patience can indulge in the useful and pleasant art.

During our waking hours on Earth our ego is confined to the physical body, and unless one is trained it is not possible to separate them. When we sleep it is only the physical body which needs rest, the spirit disengages itself and usually goes to the spirit realm in much the same way as a child returns home at the end of the school day. The ego and physical bodies maintain contact by means of the "silver cord", which is capable of unlimited extension. The body stays alive so long as the silver cord is intact; at death the cord is severed as the spirit is born into another life in the spirit world, just as a baby's umbilical cord is severed to part it from its mother. Birth, to a baby, is death to the sheltered life it led within the mother's body. Death, to the spirit, is birth again into the freer world of spirit. While the silver cord is intact, the ego is free to roam during sleep, or consciously in the case of those specially trained. The roaming of the spirit produces dreams, which are impressions transmitted along the silver cord. As the physical mind receives them they are "rationalized" to fit in with one's earth belief. In the world of spirit there is no time—"time" is a purely physical concept—and so we have cases where long and involved dreams seem to occur in the fraction of a second. Probably everyone has had a dream in which a person far away, perhaps across the oceans, has been met and spoken to. Some message may have been given, and on awakening there is usually a strong impression of *something* that should be remembered. Frequently there is the memory of meeting a distant friend or relative and it is no surprise to hear from that person within a very short time. In those who are untrained the memory is often distorted and the result is an illogical dream or nightmare.

In Tibet we travel much by astral projection—not by levitation —and the whole process is within our control. The ego is made to leave the physical body, although still connected to it by the silver cord. One can travel where one wills, as quickly as one can think. Most people have the ability to engage in astral travel. Many have actually started out, and being untrained, have experienced a shock. Probably everyone has had the sensation of just drifting off to sleep and then, without apparent reason, being violently awakened by a sudden powerful jerk. This is caused by too rapid exteriorization of the ego, an ungentle parting of physical and astral bodies. It causes contraction of the silver cord, and the astral is snatched back into the physical vehicle. It is a much worse feeling when one has travelled and is returning. The astral is floating many feet above the body, like a balloon at the end of a string. Something, perhaps some external noise, causes the astral to return to the body with excessive rapidity. The body awakens suddenly, and there is the horrible feeling that one has fallen off a cliff and awakened just in time.

Astral travelling, under one's full control, and while fully conscious, can be accomplished by almost anyone. It needs practice, but above all, in the early stages, it demands privacy, where one can be alone without fear of interruption. This is not a textbook of metaphysics, so there is no point in giving instructions on astral travelling, but it should be emphasized that it can be a disturbing experience unless one has a suitable teacher. There is no actual danger, but there is a risk of shocks and emotional disturbances if the astral body is allowed to leave or return to the physical body out of phase or coincidence. People with heart weaknesses should *never* practise astral projection. While there is no danger in projection itself, there *is* grave danger—to those with a weak heart— if another person enters the room and disturbs the body or cord. The resulting shock could prove fatal, and this would be very inconvenient indeed as the ego would have to be reborn to finish that particular span of life before it could progress to the next stage.

We Tibetans believe that everyone before the Fall of Man had the ability to travel in the astral, see by clairvoyance, telepathize, and levitate. Our version of that Fall is that Man abused the occult powers and used them for self-interest instead of for the development of mankind as a whole. In the earliest days mankind could converse with mankind by telepathy. Local tribes had their own versions of vocal speech which they used exclusively among themselves. The telepathic speech was, of course, by thought, and could be understood by all, regardless of local language. When the power of telepathy was lost, through abuse, there was—Babel!

We do not have a "Sabbath" day as such: ours are "Holy Days" and are observed on the eighth and fifteenth of each month. Then there are special services and the days are regarded as sacred and no work is normally done. Our annual festivals, I have been told, correspond somewhat to the Christian festivals, but my knowledge of the latter is quite insufficient for me to comment. Our festivals are:

First month, this corresponds roughly to February, from the first to the third day we celebrate Logsar. This, in the Western world, would be called the New Year. It is a great occasion for games as well as religious services. Our greatest ceremony of the whole year is held from the fourth to the fifteenth day, these are the "Days of Supplication". Our name for it is *Mon-lam*. This ceremony really is the highlight of the religious and secular year. On the fifteenth day of this same month we have the Anniversary of Buddha's Conception. This is not a time for games, but one of solemn thanksgiving. To complete the month, we have, on the twenty-seventh, a celebration which is partly religious, partly mythical. It is the Procession of the Holy Dagger. With that, the events of the first month are ended.

The second month, which approximates to March, is fairly free of ceremony. On the twenty-ninth day there is the Chase and Expulsion of the Demon of Ill-luck. The third month, April, also has very few public ceremonies. On the fifteenth day there is the Anniversary of Revelation.

With the arrival of the eighth day of the fourth month, May by the Western calendar, we celebrate the Anniversary of Buddha's Renunciation of the World. This, so far as I understand, is similar to the Christian Lent. We had to live even more austerely during the days of Renunciation. The fifteenth day was the Anniversary of Buddha's Death. We regarded it as the anniversary of all those who had left this life. "All Souls' Day" was another term for it. On that day we burned our sticks of incense to call the spirits of those who wandered earthbound.

It will be understood that these are merely the major festivals, there are many minor days which had to be marked, and ceremonies attended, but which are not of sufficient importance to enumerate here.

June was the month when, on the fifth day, we "medical lamas" had to attend special ceremonies at other lamaseries. The celebrations were of Thanks for the Ministrations of the Medical Monks, of which Buddha was the founder. On that day we could do no wrong, but on the day after we were certainly called to account for what our superiors imagined we had done!

The Anniversary of Buddha's Birth came on the fourth day of the sixth month, July. Then also we celebrated the First Preaching of the Law.

Harvest Festival was on the eighth day of the eighth month, October. Because Tibet is an arid country, very dry, we depended upon the rivers to a much greater extent than in other countries. Rainfall was slight in Tibet, so we combined Harvest Festival with a Water Festival, as without water from the rivers there would be no harvest from the land.

The twenty-second day of the ninth month, November, was the anniversary of Buddha's Miraculous Descent from Heaven. The next month, the tenth, we celebrated the Feast of the Lamps on the twenty-fifth day.

The final religious events of the year were on the twenty-ninth to thirtieth days of the twelfth month, which is the junction of January and February according to the Western calendar. At this time we had the Expulsion of the Old Year, and making ready for the new.

Our calendar is very different indeed from the Western: we use a sixty-year cycle and each year is indicated by twelve animals and five elements in various combinations. The New Year is in February. Here is the Year Calendar for the present Cycle which started in 1927:

1927 the Year of the Fire Hare;
1928 the Year of the Earth Dragon;
1929 the Year of the Earth Serpent;
1930 the Year of the Iron Horse;
1931 the Year of the Iron Sheep;
1932 the Year of the Water Ape;
1933 the Year of the Water Bird;
1934 the Year of the Wood Dog;
1935 the Year of the Wood Hog;
1936 the Year of the Fire Mouse;
1937 the Year of the Fire Ox;
1938 the Year of the Earth Tiger;
1939 the Year of the Earth Hare;
1940 the Year of the Iron Dragon;
1941 the Year of the Iron Serpent;
1942 the Year of the Water Horse;
1943 the Year of the Water Sheep;
1944 the Year of the Wood Ape;
1945 the Year of the Wood Bird;
1946 the Year of the Fire Dog;
1947 the Year of the Fire Hog;
1948 the Year of the Earth Mouse;
1949 the Year of the Earth Ox;
1950 the Year of the Iron Tiger;
1951 the Year of the Iron Hare;
1952 the Year of the Water Dragon;
1953 the Year of the Water Serpent;
1954 the Year of the Wood Horse;
1955 the Year of the Wood Sheep;
1956 the Year of the Fire Ape;
1957 the Year of the Fire Bird;

1958 the Year of the Earth Dog;
1959 the Year of the Earth Hog;
1960 the Year of the Iron Mouse;
1961 the Year of the Iron Ox;
      and so on.

It is part of our belief that the probabilities of the future can be foretold. To us, divination, by whatever means, is a science and is

The Prophecy.

།། དབང་ཐང་བསྟན་སྲད་གཉོ་ལོ་ཤིང་པོ་འཁྲུག

།ལོ་སྟོང་རྒྱལ་པོ་གཅེན་ནུའི་སྐྱོང༌།

།ཚེམ་རྒུན་ཞེན་ཆེ་རྩོ་ད་འཁྲུག་ཁོང༌།

།དགུ་རྒུན་ལ་སོགས་འཆེར་བ་མད༌།

།མཆོན་གི་ཕྲག་བསྒལ་སྐུ་ཚོགས་འཁྲུང༌།

།ཆ་ད་བམས་སྐུ་རྒྱལ་ཕ་བུ་འཕྲུག

།ལོ་སྐྱོང་གཡུལ་རྒྱལ་སྐུན་དགའ་མཁན༎

accurate. We believe in astrology. To us "astrological influences" are but cosmic rays which are "coloured" or altered by the nature of the body reflecting them to Earth. Anyone will agree that one can have a camera, and a white light and take a picture of something. By putting various filters over the camera lens—or over the light—we can arrange for certain effects on the finished photograph. We can get orthochromatic, panchromatic, or infra-red effects, to mention three out of a large number. People are affected in a similar way by the cosmic radiation impinging upon their own chemical and electrical personality.

Buddha says: "Stargazing and astrology, forecasting lucky or unfortunate events by signs, prognosticating good or evil, all these things are forbidden." But, a later Decree in one of our Sacred Books says: "That power which is given to the few by nature, and for which that individual endures pain and suffering, that may be used. No psychic power may be used for personal gain, for worldly ambition, or as proof of the reality of such powers. Only thus can those not so gifted be protected." My Attainment of the Third Eye had been painful, and it had increased the power with which I had been born. But in a later chapter we will return to the Opening of Third Eye. Here is a good place to mention more of astrology, and quote the names of three eminent Englishmen who have seen an astrological prophecy which came true.

Since 1027 all major decisions in Tibet have been taken with the aid of astrology. The invasion of my country by the British in 1904 was accurately foretold. On page 109 is a reproduction of the actual prophecy in the Tibetan language. It reads: "In the Year of the Wood Dragon. The first part of the year protects the Dalai Lama, after that fighting and quarrelling robbers come forward. There are many enemies, troublous grief by weapons will arise, and the people will fight. At the end of the year a conciliatory speaker will end the war." That was written before the year 1850, and concerns the year 1904, the "Wood-Dragon War". Colonel Younghusband was in charge of the British Forces. He saw the Prediction at Lhasa. A Mr. L. A. Waddell, also of the British Army, saw the printed Prediction in the year 1902. Mr. Charles Bell, who later went to Lhasa, also saw it. Some other events which were accurately forecast were: 1910, Chinese Invasion of Tibet; 1911, Chinese Revolution and formation of the Nationalist Government; late 1911, eviction of Chinese from Tibet; 1914, war between England and Germany; 1933, passing from this life of the Dalai Lama; 1935, return of a fresh Incarnation of the Dalai Lama; 1950, "Evil forces would invade Tibet". The Communists invaded Tibet in October 1950. Mr. Bell, later Sir Charles Bell, saw all those predictions in Lhasa. In my own case, *everything* foretold about me has come true. Especially the hardships.

The Science—for science it is—of preparing a horoscope is not one which can be dealt with in a few pages of a book of this nature. Briefly, it consists of preparing a map of the heavens as they were at the time of conception and at the time of birth. The exact hour of birth has to be known, and that time has to be translated into "star time", which is quite different from all the zone times of the world. As the speed of the Earth in its orbit is nineteen miles a second, it will be seen that inaccuracy will make a tremendous difference. At the equator the rotational speed of the Earth is about one thousand and forty miles an hour. The world is tilted as it rolls, and the North Pole is about three thousand one hundred miles ahead of the South Pole in the autumn, but in spring the position is reversed. The longitude of the place of birth thus is of vital importance.

When the maps are prepared, those with the necessary training can interpret their meanings. The interrelationships of each and every planet has to be assessed, and the effect on the particular map calculated. We prepare a Conception Chart to know the influences in force during the very first moments of a person's existence. The Birth Map indicates the influences in force at the moment the individual enters upon an unsuspecting world. To know of the *future*—we prepare a map of the time for which it is desired to have the reading, and compare it with the Natal Chart. Some people say: "But can you *really* predict who is going to win the 2.30?" The answer is *no*! Not without casting the horoscope for every man, horse, and horse-owner concerned in the race. Closed eyes and a pin jabbing the starting list is the best method here. We *can* tell if a person will recover from an illness, or if Tom will marry Mary and live happily ever afterwards, but that deals with individuals. We can also say that if England and America do not check Communism, a war will start in the Year of the Wood Dragon, which in this cycle, is 1964. Then in that case, at the end of the century, there should be an attractive firework display to entertain any observers on Mars or Venus. Assuming that the Communists remain unchecked.

A further point which often seems to puzzle those of the Western world is the question of tracing one's past lives. People who have no skill in the matter say that it cannot be done, just as a totally deaf man might say: "I hear no sound, therefore there *is* no sound." It is possible to trace previous lives. It takes time, much working out of charts and calculations. A person may stand at an airport and wonder about the last calls of arriving aircraft. The onlookers perhaps can make a guess, but the control tower staff, with their specialized knowledge can *say*. If an ordinary sightseer has a list of aircraft registration letters and numbers, and a good timetable, he may be able to work out the ports of call himself. So can we with past lives. It would need a complete book at least to make the process clear and so it would be useless to delve more deeply now. It may be of interest to say what points Tibetan astrology covers.

We use nineteen symbols in the twelve Houses of Astrology. Those symbols indicate:

Personality and self-interest;
Finances, how one can gain or lose money;
Relations, short journeys, mental and writing ability;
Property and the conditions at the close of life;
Children, pleasures and speculations;
Illness, work, and small animals;
Partnerships, marriage, enemies and lawsuits;
Legacies;
Long journeys and psychic matters;
Profession and honours;
Friendships and ambitions;
Troubles, restraints, and occult sorrows.

We can also tell the approximate time, or under what conditions, the following incidents will occur:

Love, the type of person and the time of meeting;
Marriage, when, and how it will work out;
Passion, the "furious temper" kind;
Catastrophe, and how it will occur, or *if* it will;
Fatality;
Death, when and how;
Prison, or other forms of restraint;
Discord, usually family or business quarrels;
Spirit, the stage of evolution reached.

Although I do astrology quite a lot, I find psychometry and "crystal gazing" much more rapid and no whit less accurate. It is also easier when one is bad at figures! Psychometry is the art of picking up faint impressions of past events from an article. Everyone has this ability to some extent. People enter an old church or temple, hallowed by the passing years, and will say: "What a calm, soothing atmosphere!" But the same people will visit the site of a gruesome murder and exclaim: "Oh! I don't like it here, it is eerie, let's get out."

Crystal gazing is somewhat different. The "glass"—as mentioned above—is merely a focus for the rays from the Third Eye in much the same way as X-rays are brought to focus on a screen, and show a fluorescent picture. There is no magic at all involved, it is merely a matter of utilizing natural laws.

In Tibet we have monuments to "natural laws". Our chortens, which range in size from five feet to fifty feet high, are symbols which compare with a crucifix, or ikon. All over Tibet these chortens stand. On the sketch map of Lhasa five are shown, the Pargo Kaling is the largest, and is one of the gates of the city.

Chortens are always of the shape shown in the illustration below. The square indicates the solid foundation of Earth. Upon it rests the Globe of Water, surmounted by a Cone of Fire. Above this is a Saucer of Air, and higher, the wavering Spirit (Ether) which is waiting to leave the world of materialism. Each element is reached by way of the Steps of Attainment. The whole symbolizes the Tibetan belief. We come to Earth when we are born. During our life we climb upwards, or try to, by way of the Steps of Attainment. Eventually, our breath fails, and we enter into the spirit. Then, after a varying interval, we are reborn, to learn

SYMBOLISM OF TIBETAN CHORTENS

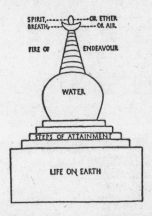

another lesson. The Wheel of Life symbolizes the endless round of birth-life-death-spirit-birth-life, and so on. Many ardent students make the serious mistake of thinking that we *believe* in those horrid hells sometimes pictured on the Wheel. A few illiterate savages may, but not those who have received enlightenment. Do Christians really believe that when they die Satan and Company get busy with the roasting and racking? Do they believe that if they go to the Other Place (being one of the minority!) they sit on a cloud in a nightshirt and take lessons in harp-playing? We believe that we learn *on Earth*, and that *on Earth* we get our "roasting and racking". The Other Place, to us, is where we go when out of the body, where we can meet entities who also are out of the body. This is not spiritualism. It is instead a belief that during sleep, or after death, we are free to wander in astral planes. Our own term for the higher reaches of these planes is "The Land of the Golden Light". We are *sure* that when we are in the astral, after death, or when asleep, we can meet those we love, because we are in harmony with them. We cannot meet those we dislike, because that would be a state of disharmony, and such conditions cannot exist in the Land of the Golden Light.

All these things have been proved by time, and it does seem rather a pity that Western doubt and materialism have prevented the Science from being *properly* investigated. Too many things have been scoffed at in the past, and then proved right by the passage of the years. Telephones, radio, television, flying, and many more.

CHAPTER ELEVEN

TRAPPA

MY youthful determination was devoted to passing the examination at the first attempt. As the date of my twelfth birthday approached, I gradually slackened off studies, for the examination started on the day after my birthday. The past years had been filled with intensive studies. Astrology, herbal medicine, anatomy, religious ethics, and even on the correct compounding of incense. Tibetan and Chinese languages, with special reference to good calligraphy, and mathematics. There had been little time for games, the only "game" we had time for was judo, because we had a stiff examination on this subject. About three months before, the Lama Mingyar Dondup had said: "Not so much revision, Lobsang, it merely clutters up the memory. Be quite calm, as you are now, and the knowledge will be there."

So the day arrived. At six in the morning I and fifteen other candidates presented ourselves at the examination hall. We had a short service to put us in the right frame of mind, and then, to make sure that none of us had yielded to unpriestly temptation, we had to strip and be searched, after which we were given clean robes. The Chief Examiner led the way from the little temple of the examination hall to the closed cubicles. These were stone boxes about six feet by ten feet in size and about eight feet high. Outside the boxes police-monks patrolled all the time. Each of us was led to a cubicle and told to enter. The door was shut, locked and a seal applied. When all of us had been sealed into our own little box, monks brought writing materials and the first set of questions to a small trap in the wall. We were also brought buttered tea and tsampa. The monk who brought that told us that we could have tsampa three times a day, and tea as often as we wanted. Then we were left to deal with the first paper. One subject a day for six days, and we had to work from the first light in the morning until it was too dark to see at night. Our cubicles had no roof, so we got whatever light came into the main examination hall.

We stayed in our own separate boxes all the time, for no reason whatever were we permitted to leave. As the evening light began to fade, a monk appeared at the trap and demanded our papers. We then lay down to sleep until the following morning. From my own experience I can say that an examination paper on one subject, which takes fourteen hours to answer, certainly does test one's knowledge and nerves. On the night of the sixth day the written examinations were at an end. We were kept in our cubicles that night because in the morning we had to clean them out and leave them as we found them. The rest of the day was ours to spend as we desired. Three days after, when our written work had been checked, and our weaknesses noted, we were called before the examiners, one at a time. They asked us questions based on our weak points only, and their interrogation occupied the whole of the day.

The next morning the sixteen of us had to go to the room where we were taught judo. This time we were going to be examined on our knowledge of strangleholds, locks, breakfalls, throws, and self-control. Each of us had to engage with three other candidates. The failures were soon weeded out. Gradually the others were eliminated, and at last, due solely to my early training at the hands of Tzu, I was the only one left. I, at least, had passed top in judo! But only because of my early training, which at the time I had thought brutal and unfair.

We were given the next day to recover from the hard days of examination, and on the day following we were informed of the results. I and four others had passed. We would now become trappas, or medical priests. The Lama Mingyar Dondup, whom I had not seen during the whole time of the examinations, sent for me to go to his room. As I entered he beamed upon me: "You have done well, Lobsang. You are at the top of the list. The Lord Abbot has sent a special report to the Inmost One. He wanted to suggest that you be made a lama right away, but I have opposed it." He saw my rather pained look, and explained: "It is much better to study and pass on your own merits. To be given the status is to miss much training, training which you will find vital in later

116

life. However, you can move into the room next to mine, because you *will* pass the examination when the time comes."

That seemed fair enough to me; I was quite willing to do whatever my Guide thought best. It gave me a thrill to realize that my success was his success, that he would get the credit for training me to pass as the highest in all subjects.

Later in the week a gasping messenger, tongue protruding, and almost at the point of death—apparently!—arrived with a message from the Inmost One. Messengers always used their histrionic talents to impress upon one the speed with which they had travelled and the hardships they had endured to deliver the message entrusted to them. As the Potala was only a mile or so away I thought, his "act" rather overdone.

The Inmost One congratulated me on my pass, and said that I was to be regarded as a lama from that date. I was to wear lama robes, and have all the right and privileges of that status. He agreed with my Guide that I should take the examinations when I was sixteen years of age, "as in this way you will be induced to study those things which you would otherwise avoid, and so your knowledge will be increased by such studying".

Now that I was a lama I should have more freedom to study without being held back by a class. It also meant that anyone with specialized knowledge was free to teach me, so I could learn as quickly as I wished.

One of the earliest things I had to learn was the art of relaxation, without which no real study of metaphysics can be undertaken. One day the Lama Mingyar Dondup came into the room where I was studying some books. He looked at me and said: "Lobsang, you are looking quite tense. You will not progress at peaceful contemplation unless you relax. I will show you how I do it."

He told me to lie down as a start, for although one can relax sitting or even standing up, it is better to learn first by being supine. "Imagine you have fallen off a cliff," he said. "Imagine that you are on the ground below, a crumpled figure with all muscles slack, with limbs bent as they have fallen and with your mouth slightly open, for only then are the cheek muscles at ease." I fidgeted around until I had put myself in the position he wanted. "Now imagine that your arms and legs are full of little people who make you work by pulling on muscles. Tell those little people to leave your feet so that there is no feeling, no movement, no tension there. Let your mind explore your feet to be certain that no muscles are being used." I lay there trying to imagine little people. Think of Old Tzu wiggling my toes from the inside! Oh, I'll be glad to get rid of him. "Then do the same with your legs. The calves; you must have a lot of little people at work there, Lobsang. They were hard at work this morning when you were jumping. Now give them a rest. March them up towards your head. Are they all out? Are you *sure*? Feel around with your mind. Make them leave the muscles untended, so that they are slack and flaccid." Suddenly he stopped and pointed: "Look!" he said, "you have forgotten someone in your thigh. A little man is keeping a tight muscle in your upper leg. Get him out, Lobsang, get him out." Finally my legs were relaxed to his satisfaction.

"Now do the same with your arms," he said, "starting with your fingers. Make them leave, up past the wrists, march them to the elbows, to the shoulders. Imagine that you are calling away all those little people so that there is no longer any strain or tension or feeling." After I had got so far he said: "Now we come to the body itself. Pretend that your body is a lamasery. Think of all the monks inside pulling on muscles to make you work. Tell them to leave. See that they leave the lower part of the body first, after slackening off all the muscles. Make them drop what they are doing and *leave*. Make them loosen your muscles, all your muscles, so that your body is held together merely by the outer covering, so that everything sags and droops and finds its own level. Then your body is relaxed."

Apparently he was satisfied with my stage of progress, for he continued: "The head is perhaps the most important part for relaxation. Let us see what we can do with it. Look at your mouth, you have a tight muscle at each corner. Ease it off, Lobsang, ease it off each side. You are not going to speak or eat, so no tension, please. Your eyes are screwed up. There is no light to trouble them, so just lightly close the lids, just lightly, without any tension." He turned away and looked out of the open window. "Our finest exponent of relaxation is outside sunning herself. You could take a lesson from the way in which a cat relaxes, there is none who can do it better."

It takes quite a long time to write this, and it seems difficult when it is read, but with just a little practice it is a simple matter to relax within a second. This system of relaxation is one which never fails. Those who are tense with the cares of civilization would do well to practise on these lines, and the mental system which follows. For this latter I was advised to proceed somewhat differently. The Lama Mingyar Dondup said: "There is little gain in being at ease physically if you are tense mentally. As you lie here physically relaxed, let your mind for a moment dwell on your thoughts. Idly follow those thoughts and see what they are. See how trivial they are. Then stop them, permit no more thoughts to flow.

118

Imagine a black square of nothingness, with the thoughts trying to jump from one side to the other. At first some will jump across. Go after them, bring them back, and make them jump back across the black space. Really imagine it, visualize it strongly, and in a very short time you will 'see' blackness without effort and so enjoy perfect mental and physical relaxation."

Here again it is far more difficult to explain than do. It really is a very simple affair with slight practice, and one must have relaxation. Many people have never shut off their mind and thoughts and they are like the people who try to keep going physically day and night. A person who tried to walk without rest for a few days and nights would soon collapse, yet the brain and mind are given no rest. With us everything was done to train the mind. We were taught judo to a high standard as an exercise in self-control. The lama who taught us judo could repel and defeat ten attackers at once. He loved judo, and went out of his way to make the subject as interesting as possible. "Strangle holds" may seem savage and cruel to Western minds, but such an impression would be utterly wrong. As I have already shown, by giving a certain little touch to the neck we could make a person unconscious in a fraction of a second, before he knew he was losing consciousness. The little pressure paralysed the brain harmlessly. In Tibet, where there are no anaesthetics, we often used that pressure when extracting a difficult tooth, or in setting bones. The patient knew nothing, suffered nothing. It is also used in initiations when the ego is released from the body to do astral travelling.

With this training we were almost immune to falls. Part of judo is to know how to land gently, "breakfalls" it is termed, and it was a common exercise for us boys to jump off a ten- or fifteen-foot wall just for fun.

Every other day, before starting our judo practice, we had to recite the Steps of the Middle Way, the keystones of Buddhism; these are:

Right Views: which are views and opinions free from delusions and self-seeking.

Right Aspirations: by which one shall have high and worthy intentions and opinions.

Right Speech: in which one is kind, considerate, and truthful.

Right Conduct: this makes one peaceful, honest, and self-less.

Right Livelihood: to obey this, one must avoid hurting men or animals, and must give the latter their rights as beings.

Right Effort: one must have self-control, and undergo constant self-training.

Right Mindfulness: in having the right thoughts and in trying to do that which is known to be right.

Right Rapture: this is the pleasure derived from meditating on the realities of life and on the Overself.

If any of us offended against the Steps we had to lie face down across the main entrance to the temple, so that all who entered had to step over the body. Here we would stay from the first dawn until dark, with no movement, and no food or drink. It was considered to be a great disgrace.

Now I was a lama. One of the élite. One of the "Superior Ones". It sounded just fine. But there were catches: before I had to obey the frightening number of thirty-two Rules of Priestly Conduct. As a lama, to my horror and dismay, I found that the total was two hundred and fifty-three. And at Chakpori the wise lama did *not* break any of those Rules! It seemed to me that the world was so full of things to learn, I thought my head would burst. But it was pleasant to sit up on the roof and watch the Dalai Lama arrive at the Norbu Linga, or Jewel Park, just down below. I had to keep hidden when I so watched the Precious One, for no one must look down on him. Down below, too, but on the other side of our Iron Mountain, I could look on two beautiful parks, the Khati Linga, and just across the stream, called the Kaling Chu, the Dodpal Linga. "Linga" means "park", or at least it is the nearest spelling according to the Western style of writing. More to the north I could gaze upon the Western Gate, the Pargo Kaling. This great chorten straddled across the road leading from Drepung, past the village of Shö, and on to the heart of the city. Nearer, almost at the foot of the Chakpori, was a chorten commemorating one of our historical heroes, King Kesar, who lived in the warlike days before Buddhism and peace came to Tibet.

Work? We had plenty of that, but we had our compensations, our pleasures as well. It was compensation in full, and brimming over, to associate with men like the Lama Mingyar Dondup. Men whose sole thought was "Peace", and help for others. It was payment, too, to be able to look over this beautiful valley so green and peopled with well-loved trees. To see the blue waters meandering through the land between the mountain ranges, to see the gleaming chortens, the picturesque lamaseries and hermitages perched on inaccessible crags. To look, with reverence, on the golden domes of the Potala so near to us, and the shining roofs of the Jo-Kang a little farther to the east. The comradeship of others, the rough good-fellowship of the lesser monks, and the familiar scent of incense as it wafted around the temples—these things made up our life, and it was a life worth living. Hardship? Yes, there was plenty. But it was worth it; in any community there are those of little understanding, of little faith: but here at Chakpori they were indeed in the minority.

CHAPTER TWELVE

HERBS AND KITES

THE weeks flew by. There was so much to do, to learn, and to plan. Now I could delve far more deeply into occult matters and receive special training. One day in early August, my Guide said: "This year we will go with the herb gatherers. You will gain much useful knowledge of herbs in their natural state, and we will introduce you to *real* kite flying!" For two weeks everyone was busy, leather bags had to be made, and the old ones cleaned. Tents had to be overhauled, and the animals carefully examined to see that they were fit and able to undertake the long trip. Our party was to be two hundred monks and we would make our base at the old Lamasery of Tra Yerpa and send out parties every day to search the neighbourhood for herbs. At the end of August we set out amid much shouting and noise. Those who were to remain behind clustered around the walls, envious of the ones going to holiday and adventure. As a lama I now rode a white horse. A few of us were going to press on with the minimum of equipment so that we could have several days at Tra Yerpa before the others arrived. Our horses would travel fifteen to twenty miles a day, but the yaks rarely exceeded eight to ten miles a day. We were lightly loaded, as we took the minimum of equipment, preferring to arrive quickly. The yak train which followed more slowly had each animal carrying the usual hundred and seventy pound load.

The twenty-seven of us who were the advance party were glad indeed to arrive at the lamasery several days later. The road had been a difficult one, and I for one was not at all fond of horse-riding. By now I could stay on even when the horse galloped, but there my prowess ended. Never could I stand on a saddle as some of the others did: I sat and clung, and if it was not graceful, then at least it was safe. We had been sighted approaching up the mountain-side, and the monks who lived there permanently prepared huge quantities of buttered tea, tsampa and vegetables. It was not entirely unselfish of them, they were anxious to have all the news of Lhasa and to receive the customary gifts which we brought. Up on the flat roof of the temple building, braziers of incense threw dense columns of smoke into the air. Up into the courtyard we rode, with new-found energy at the thought of the end of the journey. Most of the other lamas had old friends to meet. Everyone seemed to know the Lama Mingyar Dondup. He was swept from my sight by the welcoming throng, and I thought that once again I was all alone in the world, but after only a very few minutes I heard: "Lobsang, Lobsang, where are you?" I soon answered and before I knew what was happening the crowd had opened and more or less engulfed me. My Guide was talking to an elderly abbot, who turned and said: "So this is he? Well, well, well, and so young, too!"

My main concern as usual was food, and without wasting more time, everyone moved in the direction of the refectory, where we sat and ate in silence, as if we were still at Chakpori. There was some doubt as to whether Chakpori was a branch of Tra Yerpa, or the other way about. Certainly both lamaseries were amongst the oldest in Tibet. Tra Yerpa was famed as having some really valuable manuscripts dealing with herbal cures, and I was going to be able to read them and make all the notes I needed. There was also a report on the first expedition to the Chang Tang highlands, written by the ten men who did that strange journey. But of greatest interest to me at the present time was the level tableland just near, from which we were going to launch our kites.

The land here was strange. Immense peaks jutted out of con-tinually rising ground. Flat tablelands, like terraced gardens, extended from the foot of peaks like broad steps reaching higher and higher. Some of these lower steps were rich in herbs. One form of moss found here had far greater absorptive powers than sphagnum. A small plant bearing yellow berries had amazing pain-deadening properties. The monks and boys would gather these herbs and lay them out to dry. I, as a lama, would now be able to supervise them, but for me this trip would consist mainly of practical instruction from the Lama Mingyar Dondup and herb specialists. At the present moment, as I looked around, the only thought in my mind was *kites*, man-lifting kites. Tucked away in the lamasery building behind me were bars of spruce which had been brought from a far country, for no such trees grew in Tibet, and spruce, probably from Assam, was considered as ideal for kite construction, as it would take hard knocks without fracturing and it was light and strong. After the kites were finished with, the wood would be examined and placed into store ready for the next time.

The discipline was not greatly relaxed here, we still had our midnight service, and the others at regular intervals. This, if one thought about it, was the wisest way, as it would be harder to observe our long hours later if we relaxed now. The whole of our class time was devoted to herb gathering and kite-flying.

Here, in this lamasery, clinging to the side of a mountain, we were still in daylight, while down below the ground was clothed in purple shadows, and the night wind could be heard rustling through the scant vegetation. The sun sank behind the far mountain-peaks and we, too, were in darkness. Below us the country looked like a black lake. Nowhere was there a glimmer of light. Nowhere, so far as the eye could range, was there a living creature except here in this group of holy buildings. With the going down of the sun, the night wind rose and set about the business of the gods, the dusting of the corners of Earth. As it swept along the valley below, it was trapped by the mountain-side and was channelled up through faults in the rock, to emerge into our upper air with a dull moaning boom, like a giant conch calling one to service. Around us there was the creaking and crackling of rocks moving and contracting now that the greater heat of the day had gone. Above us the stars were vivid in the dark night sky. The Old People used to say that Kesar's Legions had dropped their spears on the Floor of Heaven at the call of Buddha, and the stars were but the reflections of the lights of the Heavenly Room shining through the holes.

Suddenly a new sound was heard above the noise of the rising wind, the temple trumpets sounding the close of yet another day. Up on the roof, as I looked I could dimly discern the silhouettes of monks, their robes fluttering in the breeze as they carried out their priestly office. For us, the trumpets' call meant bedtime until midnight. Dotted around the halls and temples were little groups of monks discussing the affairs of Lhasa and of the world beyond. Discussing our beloved Dalai Lama, the greatest Incarnation of any Dalai Lama. At the sound of the Close of Day they slowly dispersed and went their separate ways to bed. Gradually the living sounds of the lamasery ceased, and there was the atmosphere of peace. I lay on my back, gazing up through a small window. For this night I was too interested to sleep or to want to sleep. The stars above, and my whole life ahead. So much of it I knew, those things which had been predicted. So much had not been said. The predictions about Tibet, why, *why* did we have to be invaded? What had *we* done, a peace-loving country with no ambitions other than to develop spiritually? *Why* did other nations covet our land? We desired nothing but that which was ours: why, then, did other people want to conquer and enslave us? All we wanted was to be left alone, to follow our own Way of Life. And I was expected to go among those who later would invade us, heal their sick, and help their wounded in a war which had not yet even started. I knew the predictions, knew the incidents and highlights, yet I had to go on like a yak upon the trail, knowing all the stops and halting-places, knowing where the grazing was bad, yet having to plod on to a known destination. But maybe a yak coming over the Ridge of Reverential Prostration thought it worth while when the first sight of the Holy City was. . .

The booming of the temple drums woke me with a start. I did not even know that I had been asleep! With an unpriestly thought in my mind I tottered to my feet, reaching with sleep-numbed hands for an elusive robe. Midnight? I shall never stay awake, hope I don't fall over the steps. Oh! How cold this place is! Two hundred and fifty-three rules to obey as a lama? Well, there is one of them broken, for I did excel myself with the violence of my thoughts in being so abruptly awakened. Out I stumbled, to join those others, also in a daze, who had arrived that day. Into the temple we went, to join in the chant and counter-chant of the service.

It has been asked: "Well, if you knew all the pitfalls and hardships which had been predicted, why could you not avoid them?" The most obvious answer to that is: "If I could have avoided the *predictions*, then the mere fact of avoidance would have proven them false!" Predictions are probabilities, they do *not* mean that Man has no free will. Far from it. A man may want to go from Darjeeling to Washington. He knows his starting-point and his destination. If he takes the trouble to consult a map, he will see certain places through which he would ordinarily pass to reach his destination. While it is possible to avoid the "certain places" it is not always wise to do so, the journey may be longer or more expensive as a result. Similarly, one may motor from London to Inverness. The wise driver consults a map and has a route itinerary from one of the motoring organizations. In so doing the driver can avoid bad roads or, where he cannot *avoid* rough surfaces, he can be prepared and can drive more slowly. So with predictions.

It does not always *pay* to take the soft and easy way. As a Buddhist, I believe in reincarnation; I believe that we come to Earth to learn. When one is at school it all seems very hard and bitter. The lessons, history, geography, arithmetic, whatever they may be, are dull, unnecessary and pointless. So it appears to us at school. When we leave we may possibly sigh for the good old school. We may be so proud of it that we wear a badge, a tie, or even a distinctive colour on a monk's robe. So with life. It is hard, bitter, and the lessons we have to learn are designed to try *us* and no one else. But when we leave school, of this Earth, perhaps we wear our school badge with pride. Certainly I hope to wear *my* halo with a jaunty air later! Shocked? No Buddhist would be. Dying is merely leaving our old, empty case, and being reborn into a better world.

With the morning light we were up and anxious to explore. The older men were wanting to meet those they had missed the night before. I wanted more than anything to see these huge man-lifting kites I had heard so much about. First we had to be shown over the lamasery so that we should know our way about. Up on the high roof we looked about at the towering peaks, and gazed down at the fearsome ravines. Far away I could see a turgid stream of yellow, laden with water-borne clay. Nearer, the streams were the blue of the sky and rippling. In quiet moments I could hear the happy tinkling of a little brook behind us as it made its swift way down the mountain-side, eager to be off and join the tumbling waters of other rivers which, in India, would become the mighty Brahmaputra River, later to join the sacred Ganges and flow into the Bay of Bengal. The sun was rising above the mountains, and the chill of the air fast vanished. Far away we could see a lone vulture swooping in search of a morning meal. By my side a respectful lama pointed out features of interest. "Respectful", because I was a ward of the well-loved Mingyar Dondup, and respectful, too, because I had the "Third Eye" and was a Proved Incarnation, or Trülku, as we term it.

It may possibly interest some to give brief details of recognizing an incarnation. The parents of a boy may, from his behaviour, think that he has more knowledge than usual, or is in possession of certain "memories" which cannot be explained by normal means. The parents will approach the abbot of a local lamasery to appoint a commission to examine the boy. Preliminary pre-life horoscopes are made, and the boy is physically examined for certain signs on the body. He should, for example, have certain peculiar marks on the hands, on the shoulder blades, and on the legs. If these signs are to be seen, search is made for some clue as to who the boy was in his previous life. It may be that a group of lamas can recognize him (as in my case), and in such event some of his last-life possessions will be available. These are produced, together with others which are in appearance identical, and the boy has to recognize *all* the articles, perhaps nine, which were his in a previous life. He should be able to do this when he is three years of age.

At three years of age a boy is considered to be too young to be influenced by his parents' previous description of the articles. If the boy is younger, so much the better. Actually, it does not matter in the least if parents do try to tell the boy how to act. They are not present during the time of choosing, and the boy has to pick perhaps nine articles from possibly thirty. Two wrongly selected make a failure. If the boy is successful, then he is brought up as a Previous Incarnation, and his education is forced. At his seventh birthday predictions of his future are read, and at that age he is deemed well able to understand everything said and implied. From my own experience I know that he does understand!

The "respectful" lama at my side no doubt had all this in mind as he pointed out the features of the district. Over there, to the right of the waterfall, was a very suitable place for gathering Noil-me-tangere, the juice of which is used to remove corns and warts, and to alleviate dropsy and jaundice. Over there, in that little lake, one could gather Polygorum Hydropiper, a weed with drooping spikes and pink flowers which grows under water. We used the leaves for curing rheumatic pains and for relief of cholera. Here we gathered the ordinary type of herbs, only the highlands would supply rare plants. Some people are interested in herbs, so here are details of some of our more common types, and the uses to which we put them. The English names, if any, are quite unknown to me, so I will give the Latin names.

Allium sativum is a very good antiseptic, it is also much used for asthma and other chest complains. Another good antiseptic, used in small doses only, is *Balsamodendron myrrha*. This was used particularly for the gums and mucous membranes. Taken internally it allays hysteria.

A tall plant with cream-coloured flowers had a juice which thoroughly discouraged insects from biting. The Latin name for the plant is *Becconia cordata*. Perhaps the insects knew that, and it was the name which frightened them off! We also had a plant which was used to dilate the pupils of the eye. *Ephedra sinica* has an action similar to atropine, and it is also very useful in cases of low blood pressure besides being one of the greatest cures in Tibet for asthma. We used the dried and powdered branches and roots.

Cholera often was unpleasant to the patient and doctor because of the odour of ulcerated surfaces. *Ligusticum levisticum* killed all odour. A special note for the ladies: the Chinese use the petals of *Hibiscus rosa-sinensis* to blacken both eyebrows and shoe leather! We use a lotion made from the boiled leaves to cool the body of feverish patients. Again for the ladies, *Lilium tigrinum* really cures ovarian neuralgia, while *Flacourtia indica* provides leaves which assist women to overcome most others of their "peculiar" complaints.

In the *Sumachs Rhus* group, the *vernicifera* provides the Chinese and Japanese with "Chinese" lacquer. We used the *glabra* for the relief of diabetes, while the *aromatica* is of help in the cases of skin disease, urinary complaints, and cystitis. Another really powerful astringent for use in bladder ulceration was made from the leaves of *Arctestaphylos uva ursi*. The Chinese prefer *Bignonia grandiflora*, from the flowers of which they make an astringent for general use. In later years, in prison camps, I found that *Polygonum bistorta* was very useful indeed in treating cases of chromatic dysentery, for which we used it in Tibet.

Ladies who had loved unwisely, but well, often made use of the astringent prepared from *Polygonum erectum*. A very useful method of securing abortion. For others who had been burned, we could apply a "new skin". *Siegesbeckia orientalis* is a tall plant, some four feet high. The flowers are yellow. The juice applied to wounds and burns forms a new skin in much the same way as collodion. Taken internally, the juice had an action similar to camomile. We used to coagulate the blood of wounds with *Piper augustifolium*. The underside of the heart-shaped leaves is most efficient for the purpose. All these are very common herbs, most of the others have no Latin names, because they are not known to the Western world which bestows these designations. I mention them here merely to indicate that we had some knowledge of herbal medicine!

From our vantage-point, looking out over the countryside, we could see, on this bright, sunlit day, the valleys and sheltered places where all these plants grew. Farther out, as we gazed beyond this small area, we could see the land becoming more and more desolate. I was told that the other side of the peak upon whose side the lamasery nestled, was truly an arid region. All this I should be able to see for myself when later in the week I soared high above in a man-lifting kite.

Later in the morning the Lama Mingyar Dondup called for me and said: "Come along, Lobsang, we will go with the others who are about to inspect the kite-launching site. This should be *your* Big Day!" It needed no further remarks to get me to my feet, eager to be off. Down at the main entrance a group of red-robed monks waited for us, and together we walked down the steps and along the draughty tableland.

There was not much vegetation up here, the ground was of beaten earth over a solid rock shelf. A few sparse bushes clung to the side of the rock as if afraid of sliding over the edge and down into the ravine below. Up above us, on the roof of the lamasery, prayer-flags were held stiff and rigid by the wind, every now and then the masts creaked and groaned with the strain as they had done for ages past, and held. Near by, a small novice idly scuffed the earth with his boot, and the force of the breeze whipped away the dust like a puff of smoke. We walked towards one rocky edge of the long tableland, the edge from which the peak soared up in a gentle slope. Our robes were pressed tight against our backs, and billowed out in front, pushing us, making it difficult not to break into a run. About twenty or thirty feet from the edge was a crevice in the ground. From it the wind shot with gale force, sometimes projecting small stones and bits of lichen into the air like speeding arrows. Wind sweeping along the valley far below was trapped by the rock formations and, piling up with no easier mode of exit, poured up at high pressure through the fault in the rock, finally to emerge at the tableland with a shriek of power at being free again. Sometimes, during the season of gales, we were told, the noise was like the roaring of demons escaping from the deepest pit and ravening for victims. Wind surging and gusting in the ravine far below altered the pressure in the fault and the note rose and fell accordingly.

But now, on this morning, the current of air was constant. I could well believe the tales that were told of small boys walking into the blast and being blown straight off their feet, up into the air, to fall perhaps two thousand feet down to the rocks at the base of the crevice. It was a very useful spot from which to launch a kite, though, because the force was such that a kite would be able to rise straight up. We were shown this, with small kites similar to those I used to fly when I was a small boy at home. It was most surprising to hold the string and find one's arm lifted strongly by even the smallest toy kite.

We were led along the whole rocky shelf, and the very experienced men with us pointed out dangers to avoid, peaks which were known to have a treacherous downdraught of air, or those which seemed to attract one sideways. We were told that each monk who flew must carry a stone with him to which was attached a silk khata inscribed with prayers to the Gods of the Air to bless this, a newcomer to their domain. This stone had to be cast "to the winds" when one was of sufficient height. Then the "Gods of the Winds" would read the prayer as the cloth unrolled and streamed out and—so it was hoped—they would protect the kite-rider from all harm.

Back in the lamasery, there was much scurrying about as we carried out the materials with which to assemble the kites. Every-thing was carefully inspected. The spruce-wood poles were examined inch by inch to make certain that they were free from flaws or other damage. The silk with which the kites were to be covered was unrolled upon a smooth clean floor. Monks on hands and knees crept about in order carefully to test and view every square foot. With the examiners satisfied, the framework was lashed into position and little retaining wedges rammed home. This kite was of box form, about eight feet square and about ten feet long. Wings extended eight or nine feet from the two "horizontal" sides. Beneath the tips there had to be fixed bamboo half-hoops to act as skids and to protect the wings when taking off and landing. At the "floor" of the kite, which was strengthened, there was a long bamboo skid which tapered upwards like our Tibetan boots. This particular pole was as thick as my wrist and was strutted so that even with the kite at rest, there was no ground touching the silk, the skid and wing-protectors preventing it. I was not at all happy at first sight of the rope of yak hair. It looked flimsy. A vee of it was fastened to the wing-roots and reached to just in front of the skid. Two monks picked up the kite and carried it to the end of the flat tableland. It was quite a struggle lifting it over the updraught of air, and many monks had to hold it and carry it across.

First there was to be a trial; for this we were going to hold the rope and pull instead of using horses. A party of monks held the rope, and the Kite Master watched carefully. At his signal they ran as fast as they could, dragging the kite with them. It hit the air-stream from the fissure in the rock, and up into the air it leapt like a huge bird. The monks handling the rope were very experi-enced, and they soon paid out rope so that the kite could rise higher and higher. They held the line firmly, and one monk, tucking his robe around his waist, climbed the rope for about ten feet to test the lifting-power. Another followed him, and the two moved up so that a third man could try. The airlift was enough to support two grown men and one boy, but not quite enough for three men. This was not good enough for the Kite Master, so the monks hauled in the rope, making very sure that the kite avoided the rising air-currents. We all moved from the landing-area, except for the monks on the rope and two more to steady the kite as it landed. Down it came, seemingly reluctant to come to earth after having the freedom of the skies. With a soft "shissh" it slid to a standstill, with the two monks holding the wing-tips.

Under the instruction of the Kite Master we tightened the silk everywhere, driving little wooden wedges into the split poles to hold it firmly. The wings were taken off and replaced at a somewhat different angle, and the kite was tried again. This time it supported three grown men with ease, and almost lifted the small boy as well. The Kite Master said that it was satisfactory and now we could try the kite with a man-weight stone attached.

Once again the crowd of monks struggled to hold down the kite as it went across the updraught. Once again monks pulled on the rope, and up into the air jumped kite and stone. The air was turbulent, and the kite bobbed and swayed. It did queer things to my stomach as I watched and thought of being up there. The kite was brought down, and carried across to the starting-point. An experienced lama spoke to me: "I will go up first, then it will be your turn. Watch me carefully." He led me to the skid: "Observe how I put my feet here on this wood. Link both arms over this crossbar behind you. When you are airborne step down into the vee and sit on this thickened part of the rope. As you land, when you are eight to ten feet in the air, jump. It is the safest way. Now I will fly and you can watch."

This time the horses had been hitched to the rope. As the lama gave the signal, the horses were urged forward at a gallop, the kite slid forward, hit the updraught and leapt into the air. When it was a hundred feet above us, and two or three thousand feet above the rocks below, the lama slid down the rope to the vee, where he sat swaying. Higher and higher he went, a group of monks pulling on the rope and paying it out so that height could be gained. Then the lama above kicked hard on the rope as a signal, and the men began hauling in. Gradually it came lower and lower, swaying and twisting as kites will. Twenty feet, ten feet, and the lama was hanging by his hands. He let go, and as he hit ground he turned a somersault and so regained his feet. Dusting his robe with his hands, he turned to me and said: "Now it is your turn, Lobsang. Show us what you can do."

Now the time had arrived, I really did not think so much of kite-flying. Stupid idea, I thought. Dangerous. What a way to end a promising career. This is where I go back to prayers and herbs. But then I consoled myself, but only *very* slightly, by thoughts of the prediction in my case. If I was killed, the astrologers would be wrong, and they were never *that* wrong! The kite was now back at the starting-point, and I walked towards it with legs that were not as steady as I wished. To tell the truth, they were not steady at all! Nor did my voice carry the ring of conviction as I stood up on the skid, linked my arms behind the bar—I could only just reach—and said: "I'm ready." Never had I been more unready. Time seemed to stand still. The rope tightened with agonizing slowness as the horses galloped forward. A faint tremor through the framework, and suddenly a sickening lurch which almost threw me off. "My last moment on Earth," I thought, so closed my eyes, as there was no point in looking any more. Horrible swayings and bobbings did unpleasant things to my stomach. "Ah! A bad take-off into the astral," I thought. So I cautiously opened my eyes. Shock made me close them again. I was a hundred feet or more in the air. Renewed protests from my stomach made me fear imminent gastric disturbance, so I once again opened my eyes to be sure of my exact location in case of need. With my eyes open, the view was so superb that I forgot my distress and have never suffered from it since! The kite was bobbing and tipping, swaying, and rising, rising ever higher. Far away over the brow of the mountain I could see the khaki earth fissured with the unhealing wounds of Time. Nearer, there were the mountain ranges bearing the gaping scars of rock falls, some half hidden by the kindly lichen. Far, far away, the late sunlight was touching a distant lake and turning the waters to liquid gold. Above me the graceful bob and curtsey of the kite on the vagrant wind-eddies made me think of the gods at play in the heavens, while we poor Earth-bound mortals had to scrabble and struggle to stay alive, so that we could learn our lessons and finally depart in peace.

A violent heave and lurch made me think I had left my stomach hanging on the peak. I looked down, for the first time. Little red-brown dots were monks. They were growing larger. I was being hauled down. A few thousand feet lower, the little stream in the ravine went bubbling on its way. I had been, for the first time, a thousand feet or more above the Earth. The little stream was even more important; it would continue, and grow, and eventually help to swell the Bay of Bengal miles and miles away. Pilgrims would drink of its sacred waters, but now, I soared above its birthplace and felt as one with the gods.

Now the kite was swaying madly, so they pulled more quickly to steady it. I suddenly remembered that I had forgotten to slide down to the vee! All the time I had been standing on the skid. Unhooking my arms, I dropped to a sitting position, put my crossed legs and arms round the rope and slid. I hit the vee with a jerk that almost threatened to cut me in half. By that time the ground was about twenty feet away, I wasted no more time, but grasped the rope with my hands, and as the kite came into about eight feet, let go and turned a somersault in a "breakfall" as I landed. "Young man," said the Kite Master, "that was a good performance. You did well to remember and reach the vee, it would have cost you two broken legs otherwise. Now we will let some of the others try, and then you can go up again."

The next one to go up, a young monk, did better than I, he remembered to slide to the vee without delay. But when the poor fellow came to land, he alighted perfectly, and then fell flat on his face, clutching the ground, his face a greenish tinge, and was well and truly airsick. The third monk to fly was rather cocksure, he was not popular because of his continual boasting. He had been on the trip for three years past, and considered himself the best "airman" ever. Up he went in the air, perhaps five hundred feet up. Instead of sliding down to the vee, he straightened up, climbed inside the box kite, missed his footing and fell out of the tail end: one hand caught on the back cross-strut, and for seconds he hung by one hand. We saw his other hand flailing vainly trying to get a grip, then the kite bobbed, and he lost his hold and went tumbling end over end down the rocks five thousand feet below, his robe whipping and fluttering like a blood-red cloud.

The proceedings were a little dampened by this occurrence, but not enough to stop flying. The kite was hauled down and examined to see if it had sustained any damage: then I went up again. This time I slid down to the vee as soon as the kite was a hundred feet in the air. Below me I could see a party of monks climbing down the mountain-side to recover the body sprawled in a pulpy red mess across a rock. I looked up, and thought that a man standing in the box of the kite would be able to move position and alter the lift a little. I remembered the incident of the peasant's roof and the yak dung, and how I had gained lift by pulling on the kite string. "I must discuss it with my Guide," I thought.

At that moment there was a sickening sensation of falling, so fast and so unexpected that I almost let go. Down below the monks were hauling frantically on the rope. With the approach of evening, and the cooling of the rocks, the wind in the valley had become less, and the updraught from the funnel had almost stopped. There was little lift now, as I jumped at ten feet the kite gave one last lurch and tipped over on to me. I sat there on the rocky ground, with my head through the silk bottom of the kite box. I sat so still, so deep in thought, that the others imagined that I was injured. The Lama Mingyar Dondup rushed across. "If we had a strut across here," I said, "we should be able to stand on it and slightly alter the angle of the box, then we should have a little control over the lift." The Kite Master had heard me. "Yes, young man, you are right, but who would try it out?" "I would," I replied, "if my Guide would permit me." Another lama turned to me with a smile, "You are a lama in your own right, Lobsang, you do not have to ask anyone now." "Oh yes I do," was my response. "The Lama Mingyar Dondup taught me all I know, and is teaching me all the time, so it is for him to say."

The Kite Master supervised the removal of the kite, then took me to his own room. Here he had small models of various kites. One was a long thing which somewhat resembled an elongated bird. "We pushed the full-size one off the cliff many years ago; a man was in it. He flew for nearly twenty miles and then hit the side of a mountain. We have not done anything with this type since. Now here is a kite such as you envisage. A strut across here, and a holding bar there. We have one already made, the woodwork is already finished, it is in the little disused store at the far end of the block. I have not been able to get anyone to try it, and I am a little overweight." As he was about three hundred pounds in weight, this was an almost classic understatement. The Lama Mingyar Dondup had entered during the discussion. Now he said: "We will do a horoscope tonight, Lobsang, and see what the stars say about it."

The booming of the drums awakened us for the midnight service. As I was taking my place, a huge figure sidled up, looming like a small mountain out of the incense cloud. It was the Kite Master. "Did you do it?" he whispered. "Yes," I whispered back, "I can fly it the day after tomorrow." "Good," he muttered, "it will be ready." Here in the temple, with the flickering butter-lamps, and the sacred figures around the walls, it was difficult to think of the foolish monk who had fallen out of his present life. If he had not been showing off, I might not have thought of trying to stand inside the kite body and to some extent control the lift.

Here, inside the body of this temple, with the walls so brilliantly painted with holy pictures, we sat in the lotus style, each of us like a living statue of the Lord Buddha. Our seats were the square cushions two high, and they raised us some ten or twelve inches above the floor. We sat in double rows, each two rows facing each other. Our normal service came first, the Leader of the Chants, chosen for his musical knowledge and deep voice, sang the first passages; at the end of each, his voice sank lower and lower until his lungs were emptied of air. We droned the responses, certain passages of which were marked by the beating of the drums, or the ringing of our sweet-toned bells. We had to be extremely careful of our articulation, as we believed that the discipline of a lamasery can be gauged by the clarity of its singing, and the accuracy of the music. Tibetan written music would be difficult for a Westerner to follow: it consists of curves. We draw the rise and fall of the voice. This is the "basic curve". Those who wish to improvise, add their "improvements" in the form of smaller curves with the large. With the ordinary service ended, we were allowed ten minutes' rest before beginning the Service for the Dead for the monk who had passed from the world that day.

We assembled again on the given signal. The Leader on his raised throne intoned a passage from the Bardo Thödol, the Tibetan Book of the Dead. "O! Wandering ghost of the monk Kumphel-la who this day fell from the life of this world. Wander not among us, for you have departed from us this day. O! Wandering ghost of the monk Kumphel-la, we light this stick of incense to guide you that you may receive instruction as to your path through the Lost Lands and on to the Greater Reality." We would chant invitations to the ghost to come and receive enlightenment and guidance, we younger men in our high voices, and the older monks, growling the responses in very deep bass tones. Monks and lamas sitting in the main body of the hall in rows, facing each other, raising and lowering religious symbols in age-old ritual. "O! Wandering ghost, come to us that you may be guided. You see not our faces, smell not our incense, wherefor you are dead. Come! That you may be guided!" The orchestra of woodwind, drums, conches, and cymbals filled in our pauses. A human skull, inverted, was filled with red water to simulate blood, and was passed round for each monk to touch. "Your blood has spilled upon the earth, O monk who is but a wandering ghost, come that you may be freed." Rice grains, dyed a bright saffron, were cast to the east, to the west, to the north and to the south. "Where does the wandering ghost roam? To the east? Or the north. To the west? Or to the south. Food of the gods is cast to the corners of the Earth, and you eat it not, wherefor you are dead. Come, O wandering ghost that you may be freed and guided."

The deep bass drum throbbed with the rhythm of life itself, with the ordinary, deep-felt "ticking" of the human body. Other instruments broke in with all the sounds of the body. The faint rushing of the blood through veins and arteries, the muted whisper of breath in the lungs, the gurgling of body fluids on the move, and the various creakings, squeaks, and rumbles which make the music of life itself. All the faint noises of humanity. Starting off in ordinary tempo, a frightened scream from a trumpet, and the increased beat of the heart-sound. A soggy "thwack", and the sudden halting of noise. The end of life, a life violently terminated.

"O! monk that was, wandering ghost that is, our telepaths will guide you. Fear not, but lay bare your mind. Receive our teachings that we may free you. There is no death, wandering ghost, but only the life unending. Death is birth, and we call to free you for a new life."

Throughout centuries we Tibetans have developed the science of sounds. We know all the sounds of the body and can reproduce them clearly. Once heard they are never forgotten. Have *you* ever laid your head upon a pillow, at the verge of sleep, and heard the beating of your heart, the breathing of your lungs? In the Lamasery of the State Oracle they put the medium into a trance, using some of these sounds, and he is entered by a spirit. The soldier Younghusband, who was the head of the British Forces, invading Lhasa in 1904, testified to the power of these sounds, and to the fact that the Oracle actually changed appearance when in trance.

With the ending of the service we hurried back to our sleep. With the excitement of flying, and the very different air, I was almost asleep on my feet. When the morning came the Kite Master sent me a message that he would be working on the "controllable" kite, and inviting me to join him. With my Guide, I went to his workshop which he had fitted up in the old storeroom. Piles of foreign woods littered the floor, and the walls had many diagrams of kites. The special model which I was going to use was suspended from the vaulted roof. To my astonishment, the Kite Master pulled on a rope, and the kite came down to floor level—it was suspended on some sort of a pulley arrangement. At his invitation I climbed in. The floor of the box part had many struts upon which one could stand, and a cross-bar at waist level afforded a satisfactory barrier to which one could cling. We examined the kite, every inch of it. The silk was removed, and the Kite Master said that he was going to cover it with new silk himself. The wings at the sides were not straight, as on the other machine, but were curved, like a cupped hand held palm down: they were about ten feet long and I had the impression that there would be very good lifting-power.

The next day the machine was carried out into the open, and the monks had a struggle to hold it down when carrying it across the crevice with the strong updraught of air. Finally they placed it in position and I, very conscious of my importance, clambered into the box part. This time monks were going to launch the kite instead of using horses as was more usual: it was considered that monks could exercise more control. Satisfied, I called out: "*Tradri, them-pa*," (ready, pull). Then as the first tremor ran through the frame, I shouted: "*O-na-dö-a!*" (good-bye!). A sudden jolt, and the machine shot up like an arrow. A good thing I was hanging on thoroughly, I thought, or they would be searching for *my* wandering ghost tonight, and I'm quite satisfied with this body for a little longer. The monks below played with the rope, managed it skilfully, and the kite rose higher and higher. I threw out the stone with the prayer to the Wind Gods, and it just missed a monk far below: we were later able to use that cloth again as it fell at the monk's feet. Down below the Kite Master was dancing with impatience for me to start my testing, so I thought I had better get on with it. Cautiously moving around I found that I could very considerably alter the performance, the "lift" and "attitude" of the kite.

I grew careless and too confident. I moved to the back of the box—and the kite fell like a stone. My feet slipped from the bar

and I was hanging straight down by my hands, at arms' length. By great efforts, with my robe whipping and flapping around my head, I managed to draw myself up and climb to the normal position. The fall stopped, and the kite surged upwards. By then I had got my head free of my robe and I looked out. If I had not been a shaven-headed lama my hair would have stood straight on end: I was less than two hundred feet above the ground. Later, when I landed, they said I had come to fifty feet before the kite's fall was checked, and it again rose.

For a time I clung to the bar, panting and gasping with the exertion in the thin air. As I looked about over the miles and miles of countryside, I saw in the far distance something that looked like a dotted line moving along. For a moment I stared uncomprehendingly, then it dawned upon me. Of course! It was the rest of the herb-gathering party making their slow way across the desolate country. They were strung out, big dots, little dots, and long dots. Men, boys, and animals, I thought. So slowly they moved, so painfully hesitant their progress. It gave me much pleasure, upon landing, to say that the party would be with us within a day or so.

It was truly fascinating to look about over the cold blue-grey of the rocks, and the warm red ochre of the earth and see lakes shimmering in the far distance. Down below, in the ravine, where it was warmed and sheltered from the bitter winds, mosses, lichens, and plants made a carpetwork which reminded me of that in my father's study. Across it ran the little stream which sang to me in the night. Ran across it, yes, and that, too, reminded me—painfully—of the time when I upset a jar of clear water over father's carpet! Yes, my father certainly had a very heavy hand!

The country at the back of the lamasery was mountainous, peak after peak rising in their serried ranks until, against the far-distant skyline they stood outlined blackly against the sunlight. The sky in Tibet is the clearest in the world, one can see as far as the mountains will permit, and there are no heat-hazes to cause distortion. So far as I could see, nothing moved in the whole vast distance except the monks below me, and those scarce-recognizable dots toiling interminably towards us. Perhaps they could see me here. But now the kite began to jerk; the monks were hauling me down. With infinite care they pulled so as to avoid damaging the valuable experimental machine.

On the ground, the Kite Master looked on me with fond affection, and put his mighty arms around my shoulders with such enthusiasm that I was *sure* that every bone was crushed. No one else could get a word in, for years he had had "theories", but could not put them to the test, his immense bulk made it impossible for him to fly. As I kept telling him, when he paused for breath, I *liked* doing it, I got as much pleasure out of flying as he did from designing, experimenting, and watching. "Yes, yes, Lobsang, now, if we just move this over to here, and put that strut there. Yes, that will do it. Hmmm, we will take it in and start on it now. And it rocked sideways, you say, when you did this?" So it went on. Fly and alter, fly and alter. And I loved every second of it. No one but I was allowed to fly—or even set foot—in that special kite. Each time I used it there were some modifications, some improvements. The biggest improvement, I thought, was a strap to hold me in!

But the arrival of the rest of the party put a stop to kite-flying for a day or two. We had to organize the newcomers into gathering and packing groups. The less experienced monks were to gather three kinds of plants only, and they were sent to areas where such plants were plentiful. Every group stayed away for seven days, ranging the sources of supply. On the eighth day they returned with the plants, which were spread out on the clean floor of a huge storage room. Very experienced lamas examined every plant to make sure that it was free from blight, and of the right type. Some plants had the petals removed and dried. Others had the roots grated and stored. Yet others, as soon as they were brought in, were crushed between rollers for the juice. This fluid was stored in tightly sealed jars. Seeds, leaves, stems, petals, all were cleaned and packed in leather bags when quite dry. The bags would have the contents noted on the outside, the neck would be twisted to make it watertight, and the leather would be quickly dipped in water and exposed to the strong sunlight. Within a day the leather would have dried as hard as a piece of wood. So hard would a bag become, that to open it the tightly twisted end would have to be knocked off. In the dry air of Tibet, herbs stored in this way would keep for years.

After the first few days I divided my time between herb-gathering and kite-flying. The old Kite Master was a man of much influence and, as he said, in view of the predictions concerning my future, knowledge of machines in the sky were as important as the ability to gather herbs and classify them. For three days a week I flew in the kites. The rest of the time was spent in riding from group to group so that I could learn as much as possible in the shortest time. Often, high above in a kite, I would look out over the now familiar landscape and see the black yak-hide tents of the herb-gatherers. Around them the yaks would be grazing, making up for lost time, the time at the end of the week when they would have to carry in the loads of herbs. Many of these plants were quite well known in most Eastern countries, but others had not been "discovered" by the Western world and so had no Latin names. A knowledge of herbs has been of great use to me, but the knowledge of flying not less so.

We had one more accident: a monk had been watching me rather closely, and when it was his turn to fly, in an ordinary kite, he thought that he could do as well as I. High in the air the kite seemed to be acting strangely. We saw that the monk was flinging himself about in an attempt to control the position of the machine. One specially rough lurch, and the kite dipped and tilted sideways. There was a ripping and splintering of wood, and the monk came tumbling out of the side. As he fell he spun head over feet with his robe whirling over his head. A rain of articles fell down, tsampa bowl, wooden cup, rosary, and various charms. He would no longer need them. Spinning end over end, he finally disappeared in the ravine. Later, came the sound of the impact.

All good things come too quickly to an end. The days were full of work, hard work, but all too soon our three months' visit drew to a close. This was the first of a number of pleasant visits to the hills, and to the other Tra Yerpa nearer Lhasa. Reluctantly we packed our few belongings. I was given a beautiful model man-lifting kite by the Kite Master which he had made specially for me. On the next day we set off for home. A few of us, as on arriving, did a forced ride, and the main body of monks, acolytes, and pack animals followed on in leisurely manner. We were glad to be back at the Iron Mountain, but sorry indeed to be parted from our new friends and the great freedom of the hills.

CHAPTER THIRTEEN

FIRST VISIT HOME

WE had arrived back in time for the Losgar, or New Year, ceremonies. Everything had to be cleaned, everywhere tidied. On the
fifteenth day the Dalai Lama went to the Cathedral for a number
of services. With them ended, he came out for his tour of the
Barkhor, the ring road which went outside the Jo-Kang and
Council Hall, round by the market-place, and completed the
circuit between the big business houses. At this time of the celebrations, the solemnity was being replaced by jollity.The gods were
appeased, and now was the time for pleasure and enjoyment. Huge
frameworks, from thirty to forty feet high, supported images
made of coloured butter. Some of the frames had "butter pictures"
in relief of various scenes from our Sacred Books. The Dalai
Lama walked around and examined each one. The most attractive
exhibit earned for the lamasery making it the title of the best
butter modellers of the year. We of Chakpori were not at all
interested in these carnivals, it all seemed rather childish and
unamusing to us. Nor were we interested in the other proceedings
when riderless horses raced across the Plain of Lhasa in open
competition. We were more interested in the giant figures
representing characters from our legends. These figures were
constructed on a light wooden framework to represent the body, and
a very realistic huge head was fitted. Inside the head were butter-
lamps which shone through the eyes, and, in flickering, appeared
to make the eyes move from side to side. A strong monk on stilts
would be inside the frame of the figure, with his eyes giving a very
indifferent view through the giant's mid-section. All kinds of

unusual accidents would happen to these performers. The poor wretch would put one stilt in a pot-hole and find that he was balancing on one stilt, or one stilt would perhaps skid on some slippery substance on the road. One of the worst things was when the lamps were jerked loose—and set fire to the whole figure!

Once, in later years, I was persuaded to carry round the figure of Buddha the God of Medicine. It was twenty-five feet high. The flowing robes flapped round my stilted legs, moths flapped around as well, for the garments had been stored. As I jerked along the road, dust was shaken from the folds, and I sneezed and sneezed and sneezed. Every time I did so I felt that I was going to topple over. Every sneeze caused a further jerk, and added to my discomfort by spilling hot butter from the lamps over my shaven and suffering pate. The heat was terrible. Swaths of mouldy old clothes, swarms of bewildered moths, and hot butter. Normally butter in a lamp is solid with the exception of a little pool around the wick. Now, in this stifling heat, the whole lot had melted. The little peephole in the mid-section of the figure was not in line with my eyes, and I could not let go of the stilts in order to rearrange it. All I could see was the back of the figure in front of me, and by the way it was hopping about and swaying, the poor wretch inside was having a bad a time as I. However, with the Dalai Lama watching there was nothing to do but to march on, suffocated with cloth and half roasted in butter fat. With the heat and exertion I am sure that I lost pounds of weight that day! A high lama that night said: "Oh, Lobsang, your performance was *good*, you would make a very excellent *comedian*!" I certainly did not tell him that the "antics" which amused him so much were entirely involuntary. Most definitely I did not carry a figure again!

Not long after this, I think it may have been five or six months, there was a sudden terrific gale of wind, with flying clouds of dust and grit. I was on the roof of a storehouse being instructed in how to lay sheet gold to make the roof waterproof. The gale caught me and whirled me off the flat roof, to bump first on another roof some twenty feet lower. Another gust caught me and blew me over the edge and over the side of the Iron Mountain and down to the side of the Lingkhor road some three hundred and fifty feet below. The ground was swampy and I landed with my face in the water. Something snapped, another branch, I thought. Dazedly I tried to lift myself out of the mud, but found that the pain was intense when I tried to move my left arm or shoulder. Somehow I got to my knees, to my feet, and struggled along to the dry road. I felt sick with pain, and I could not think clearly, my sole thought was to get up the mountain as quickly as possible. Blindly I struggled

143

and stumbled along, until, about halfway up, I met a party of monks rushing down to see what had happened to me and to another boy. He had landed on rocks, and so was dead. I was carried up the rest of the way, to the room of my Guide. Quickly he examined me: "Oé, Oé, poor boys, they should not have been sent out in such a gale!" He looked at me: "Well, Lobsang, you have a broken arm and a broken collar-bone. We shall have to set them for you. It will hurt, but not more than I can help."

While he was talking, and almost before I knew, he had set the collar-bone and bound splinting in place to hold the broken bones. The upper arm was more painful, but soon that, too, was set and splinted. For the rest of that day I did nothing but lie down. With the arrival of the next day, the Lama Mingyar Dondup said. "We cannot let you fall behind in studies, Lobsang, so you and I will study together here. Like all of us you have a certain little dislike of learning new things, so I am going to remove that 'study antagonism' hypnotically." He closed the shutters and the room was in darkness except for the faint light from the altar lamps. From somewhere he took a small box which he stood on a shelf in front of me. I seemed to see bright lights, coloured lights, hands and bars of colour, and then all appeared to end in a silent explosion of brightness.

It must have been many hours later when I awoke. The window was again open, but the purple shadows of night were beginning to fill the valley down below. From the Potala, little lights were twinkling in and around the buildings as the evening guard went their rounds making sure that all was secure. I could look across the city where, too, the night life was now commencing. Just then, my Guide came in: "Oh!" he said, "so you have returned to us at last. We thought that you found the astral fields so pleasant that you were staying a while. Now, I suppose—as usual—you are hungry." As he mentioned it, I realized that I was, definitely. Food was soon brought, and as I ate he talked. "By ordinary laws you should have left the body, but your stars said you would live to die in the Land of the Red Indians (America) in many years' time. They are having a service for the one who did not stay. He was killed on the instant."

It appeared to me that the ones who had passed over were the lucky ones. My own experiences in astral travelling had taught me that it was very pleasant. But then I reminded myself that we did not really like school, but we had to stay to learn things, and what was life on Earth but a school? A hard one, too! I thought: "Here am I with two broken bones, and I have to go on *learning*!"

For two weeks I had even more intensive teaching than usual,

144

I was told it was to keep my mind from thinking of my broken bones. Now, at the end of the fortnight, they had united, but I was stiff, and both my shoulder and arm were painful. The Lama Mingyar Dondup was reading a letter when I went into his room one morning. He looked up at me as I entered.

"Lobsang," he said, "we have a packet of herbs to go to your Honourable Mother. You can take it tomorrow morning and stay the day."

"I am sure my father would not want to see me," I answered. "He ignored me completely when he passed me on the steps of the Potala."

"Yes, of course he did. He knew that you had just come from the Precious One, he knew that you had been specially favoured, and so he *could not* speak unless I was with you, because you are now my ward by order of the Precious One Himself." He looked at me, and the corners of his eyes crinkled as he laughed: "Anyhow, your father will not be there tomorrow. He has gone to Gyangtse for several days."

In the morning my Guide looked me over and said: "Hmm, yes, you look a little pale, but you are clean and tidy and that should count a lot with a mother! Here is a scarf, don't forget that you are now a lama and must conform to all the Rules. You came here on foot. Today you will ride on one of our best white horses. Take mine, it needs some exercise."

The leather-bag of herbs, handed to me as I left, had been wrapped in a silk scarf as a sign of respect. I looked at it dubiously, wondering how I was going to keep the wretched thing clean. In the end I took off the scarf and tucked it into my robe pouch until I was nearer home.

Down the steep hill we went, the white horse and I. Halfway down the horse stopped, turned his head round to get a good look at me. Apparently he did not think much of what he saw, because he gave a loud neigh, and hurried on as if he could not bear the sight of me any longer. I sympathized with him as I had identical opinions about him! In Tibet, the most orthodox lamas ride mules as they are supposed to be sexless affairs. Lamas who are not so finicky ride a male horse or pony. For myself, I preferred to walk if at all possible. At the bottom of the hill we turned right. I sighed with relief; the horse agreed with me that we turn right. Probably because one *always* traverses the Lingkhor road in a clockwise direction for religious reasons. So we turned *right* and crossed the Drepung-City road to continue along the Lingkhor circuit. Along past the Potala which I thought was not to be compared to our Chakpori for attractiveness, and across the road to India, leaving the Kaling Chu on our left and the Snake Temple on our right. At the entrance to my former home, a little way farther on, servants saw me coming and hastened to swing open the gates. Straight into the courtyard I rode, with a swagger and a hope that I would not fall off. A servant held the horse, fortunately, while I slid off.

Gravely the Steward and I exchanged our ceremonial scarves. "Bless this house and all that be in it, Honourable Medical Lama, Sir!" said the Steward. "May the Blessing of Buddha, the Pure One, the All-seeing One be upon you and keep your healthy," I replied. "Honourable Sir, the Mistress of the House commands me lead you to her." So off we went (as if I could not have found my own way!), with me fumbling to wrap up the bag of herbs with the wretched scarf again. Upstairs, into mother's best room. "I was never allowed here when I was merely a son," I thought. My second thought was to wonder if I should turn and run for it, the room was full of women!

Before I could, my mother came towards me and bowed, "Honourable Sir and Son, my friends are here to hear of your account of the honour conferred upon you by the Precious One."

"Honourable Mother," I replied, "the Rules of my Order prevent me from saying what the Precious One told me. The Lama Mingyar Dondup instructed me to bring you this bag of herbs and to present you with his Scarf of Greeting."

"Honourable Lama and Son, these ladies have travelled far to hear of the events of the Inmost House and of the Precious One within. Does he *really* read Indian magazines? And is it true that he has a glass which he can look through and see through the walls of a house?"

"Madam," I answered, "I am but a poor Medical Lama who has recently returned from the hills. It is not for such as I to speak of the doings of the Head of our Order. I have come only as a messenger."

A young woman came up to me and said: "Don't you remember me? I am Yaso!"

To be truthful, I hardly could recognize her, she had developed so much, and was so ornamental! . . . I had misgivings. Eight, no, nine women were too much of a problem for me. Men, now I knew how to deal with them, but *women*! They looked at me as if I were a juicy morsel and they hungry wolves on the plains. There was but one course of action: retreat.

"Honourable Mother," I said, "I have delivered my message and now I must return to my duties. I have been ill and have much to do."

With that, I bowed to them, turned, and made off as fast as I decently could. The Steward had returned to his office, and the groom brought out the horse. "Help me to mount carefully," I said, "for I have recently had an arm and a shoulder broken and cannot manage alone." The groom opened the gate, I rode out just as mother appeared on the balcony and shouted something. The white horse turned left so that we could again travel clockwise along the Lingkhor road. Slowly I rode along. Slowly, as I did not want to get back *too* quickly. Past Gyü-po Linga, past Muru Gompa, and along the complete circuit.

Once again home, on the Iron Mountain, I went to the Lama Mingyar Dondup. He looked at me: "Why, Lobsang, have all the wandering ghosts chased you around the City? You look shaken!"

"Shaken?" I answered, "*shaken*? My mother had a batch of *women* there and they all wanted to know about the Inmost One and what He said to me. I told them the Rules of the Order would not allow me to say. And I made off while I was safe, all those women staring at me! . . ."

My Guide shook and shook with laughter. The more I stared at him in amazement, the more he laughed.

"The Precious One wanted to know if you had settled down here, or if you still had thoughts of home."

Lamastic life had upset my "social" values, women were strange creatures to me (they *still* are!), and . . . "But I *am* home. Oh no, I do not want to return to the House of my Father. The sight of all those women, painted, stuff on their hair, and the way they looked at me: as if I were a prize sheep and they butchers from Shö. Screeching voices, and"—I am afraid *my* voice must have sunk to a whisper—"their astral *colours*. Dreadful! Oh, Honourable Lama Guide, do not let us discuss it!"

For days I was not allowed to forget it: "Oh, Lobsang, put to flight by a pack of women!" or, "Lobsang, I want you to go to your Honourable Mother, she has a party today and they need entertaining." But after a week I was again told that the Dalai Lama was very, very interested in me, and had arranged for me to be sent home when my mother had one of her numerous social parties. No one ever obstructed the Precious One, we all loved him, not merely as a God on Earth, but as the true Man that he was. His temper was a bit hasty, but so was mine, and he never let personal bias interfere with the duties of the State. Nor did he stay in a temper for more than minutes. He was the Supreme Head of State and Church.

CHAPTER FOURTEEN

USING THE THIRD EYE

ONE morning, when I was at peace with the world, and wondering how to fill in an idle half-hour before the next service, the Lama Mingyar Dondup came to me. "Let us take a walk, Lobsang. I have a small job for you to do." I jumped to my feet, glad to be going out with my Guide. It did not take us long to get ready, and then we set off. As we were leaving the Temple one of the cats displayed marked affection and we could not leave him until the roaring purr had stopped and the tail started to wag. This was a huge cat, we called him "cat", in Tibetan, of course, and that was *shi-mi*. Satisfied that his affection was fully reciprocated, he walked solemnly beside us until we were halfway down the mountain. Then, apparently, he remembered that he had left the jewels unguarded, and off he rushed in a very great hurry.

Our temple cats were not for ornament only, they were fierce guardians of the masses of uncut gems strewn around the holy figures. In houses dogs were the guardians, immense mastiffs who would pull a man down and savage him. These dogs could be cowed and driven off. Not so with the cats. Once they attacked, only death could stop them. They were of the type sometimes named "Siamese". Tibet is cold, so these cats were nearly black. In hot countries, so I have been told, they are white, the temperature affecting the fur colour. Their eyes were blue, and their hind legs were long, giving them a "different" appearance when they walked. Their tails were long and whip-like, and their voices! . . . No cat ever had a voice like these. The volume and range of tones was almost beyond belief.

148

On duty these cats prowled in the temples, silent-footed and alert, like dark shadows of the night. If anyone tried to reach the jewels, which were otherwise unguarded, a cat would emerge and leap at the man's arm. Unless he let go immediately, another cat would jump, perhaps from the Holy Image, straight at the thief's throat. And those cats had claws twice as long as those of the "average" cat—and they did *not* let go. Dogs could be beaten off, or perhaps held or poisoned. Not so with the cats. They would put the fiercest mastiffs to flight. Only men who personally knew those cats could approach them when they were on duty.

We sauntered on. Down at the road we turned right through the Pargo Kaling and walked on past the village of Shö. On over the Turquoise Bridge and right again at the House of Doring. This brought us to the side of the old Chinese Mission. As we walked the Lama Mingyar Dondup talked to me. "A Chinese Mission has arrived, as I told you. Let us have a look at them and see what they are like."

My first impression was a very unfavourable one. Inside the house the men were pacing about arrogantly unpacking boxes and cases. They appeared to have enough weapons to supply a small army. Being a small boy, I could "investigate" in a manner which was quite unsuitable for an older person. I crept through the grounds and silently approached an open window. For a time I stood and watched until one of the men looked up and saw me. He uttered a Chinese oath which threw grave doubts upon my ancestry, but left none whatever about my future. He reached for something, so I withdrew before he could throw it.

On the Lingkhor road again, I said to my Guide: "Oh! *How* their auras turned red! And they wave knives about so."

For the rest of the way home the Lama Mingyar Dondup was very thoughtful. After our supper he said to me: "I have been thinking quite a lot about these Chinese. I am going to suggest to the Precious One that we make use of your special abilities. Do you feel confident that you can watch them through a screen if it can be arranged?"

All I could say was: "If you think I can do it, then I can."

The next day I did not see my Guide at all, but the following day he taught me in the morning and after the midday meal said: "We will take a walk this afternoon, Lobsang. Here is a scarf of the first quality, so you do not need to be a clairvoyant to know where we are going. Ten minutes to get yourself ready and then meet me in my room. I have to go and see the Abbot first."

Once again we set off on the precipitous path down the mountain-side. We took a short cut down over the south-west side of our mountain and, after a very short walk, arrived at the Norbu Linga. The Dalai Lama was very fond of this Jewel Park and spent most of his free time there. The Potala was a beautiful place, outside, but inside it was stuffy through insufficient ventilation and too many butter-lamps burning for too long. Much butter had been spilled on the floors throughout the years, and it was not a new experience for a dignified lama to pursue his stately way down a sloping ramp, tread on a lump of butter covered in dust, and arrive at the bottom of the ramp with an "Ulp!" of astonishment, as part of his anatomy hit the stone flooring. The Dalai Lama did not wish to risk being the subject of such an unedifying spectacle, so he stayed at the Norbu Linga whenever possible.

This Jewel Park was surrounded by a stone wall some twelve feet high. The Park is only about a hundred years old. The Palace within had golden turrets and consisted of three buildings which were used for official and state work. An Inner Enclosure, which also had a high wall, was used by the Dalai Lama as a pleasure garden. Some people have written that officials were forbidden to enter this enclosure. That definitely is not so. They were forbidden to do any official business within the enclosure. I have been there some thirty times and know it well. It contained a very beautiful artificial lake with two islands, upon which there were two summer-houses. At the north-west corner a wide stone causeway enabled one to reach the islands and the summer-house on each. The Dalai Lama spent much time on one or other of these islands and spent many hours each day in meditation there. Inside the Park there were barracks which housed some five hundred men who acted as personal bodyguards. It was to this place that the Lama Mingyar Dondup was taking me. This was my first visit. We walked through the very beautiful land and through an ornamental gateway leading to the Inner Enclosure. All manner of birds were pecking food from the ground as we entered, and they took no notice of us, *we* had to get out of *their* way! The lake was placid, like a highly polished metal mirror. The stone causeway had been newly whitewashed, and we made our way to the farthest island where the Inmost One was sitting in deep meditation. At our approach he looked up and smiled. We knelt and laid our scarves at his feet and he told us to sit in front of him. He rang a bell for the buttered tea without which no Tibetan could carry out a discussion. While we were waiting for it to be brought, he told me of the various animals he had in the Park and promised that I should see them later.

With the arrival of the tea and the departure of the lama attendant, the Dalai Lama looked at me and said: "Our good friend Mingyar tells me that you do not like the auric colours of this Chinese Delegation. He says that they have many weapons upon their persons. In all the tests, secret and otherwise, upon your clairvoyance, you have never failed. What is your opinion, of these men?"

This did not make me happy, I did not like telling others—except the Lama Mingyar Dondup—what I saw in the "colours" and what they meant to me. In my reasoning, if a person could not see for himself, then he was not meant to know. But how does one say that to the Head of a State? Particularly to a Head who was not clairvoyant.

To the Dalai Lama my reply was: "Honourable Precious Protector, I am quite unskilled in the reading of foreign auras. I am unworthy to express an opinion."

This reply did not get me anywhere. The Inmost One replied: "As one possessed of special talents, further increased by the Ancient Arts, it is your duty to say. You have been trained to that end. Now say what you saw."

"Honourable Precious Protector, these men have evil intentions. The colours of their auras show treachery." That was all I said.

The Dalai Lama looked satisfied. "Good, you have repeated it as you told Mingyar. You will conceal yourself behind that screen tomorrow, and watch when the Chinese are here. We must be *sure*. Conceal yourself now, and we will see if you are adequately hidden."

I was not, so attendants were called, and the Chinese lions were shifted slightly that I might be entirely concealed. Lamas came in rehearsal as if they were the visiting delegation. They tried hard to locate my hiding-place. I caught the thought of one: "Ah! Promotion for me if I can see him!" But he did not get promotion, as he was looking on the wrong side. Eventually the Inmost One was satisfied, and called me out. He spoke for a few moments and told us to come again tomorrow, as the Chinese Delegation were going to visit him in an attempt to force a treaty upon Tibet. So with that thought before us, we took our leave of the Inmost One and wended our way up the Iron Mountain.

The following day, at about the eleventh hour, we again descended the rocky slope and made our entrance to the Inner Enclosure. The Dalai Lama smiled upon me and said that I must eat—*I* was ready for that!—before secreting myself. At his order some very palatable food was brought to the Lama Mingyar Dondup and me, comestibles imported from India in tins. I do not know what they were called, I know only that they were a very welcome change from tea, tsampa, and turnip. Well fortified, I was able to face the prospect of several hours' immobility more cheerfully. Utter immobility was a simple matter to me, and to all lamas: we had to keep still in order to meditate. From a very early age, from seven years of age to be precise, I had been taught to sit motionless for hours on end. A lighted butter-lamp used to be balanced on my head and I had to remain in the lotus attitude until the butter was finished. This could be as long as twelve hours. So now, three or four hours imposed no hardship.

Directly in front of me the Dalai Lama sat in the lotus attitude on his throne six feet above the floor. He, and I, remained motionless. From without the walls came hoarse cries, and many exclamations in Chinese. Afterwards I discovered that the Chinese had had suspicious bulges under their robes, and so had been searched for weapons. Now they were permitted to enter the Inner Enclosure. We saw them coming, being led in by the Household Guards, across the causeway and on to the porch of the Pavilion. A high lama intoned: "O! Ma-ni pad-me Hum," and the Chinamen, instead of repeating the same mantra as a courtesy, used the Chinese form: "O-mi-t'o-fo" (meaning: "Hear us, O Amida Buddha!").

I thought to myself: "Well, Lobsang, your work is easy; they show their true colours."

As I looked at them from my place of concealment I observed the shimmering of their auras, the opalescent sheen, shot with murky red. The turgid swirling of hate-filled thoughts. Bands and striations of colour, unpleasant colours, not the clear, pure shades of higher thought, but the unwholesome, contaminated hues of those whose life forces are devoted to materialism and evil-doing. They were those of whom we say: "Their speech was fair but their thoughts were foul."

I also watched the Dalai Lama. His colours indicated sadness, sadness as he remembered the past when he had been to China. All that I saw of the Inmost One I liked, the best Ruler ever of Tibet. He had a temper, quite a hot one, and then his colours *did* flash red, but history will record that there never was a better Dalai Lama, one who was utterly devoted to his country. Certainly I thought of him with very great affection, second only to the Lama Mingyar Dondup for whom I felt *more* than affection.

But the interview dragged on to its useless end, useless because these men did not come in friendship, but in enmity. Their one thought was to get their own way and not be too particular about the methods they employed. They wanted territories, they wanted to guide the policy of Tibet, and—they wanted *gold*! This latter had been a lure to them for years past. There are hundreds of tons of gold in Tibet, we regard it as a sacred metal. According to our belief, ground is desecrated when gold is mined, so it is left quite untouched. From certain streams one can pick up nuggets which have been washed down from the mountains. In the Chang Tang region I have seen gold on the sides of swift-flowing streams as sand is seen on the banks of ordinary streams. We melt down some of these nuggets, or "sand", and make temple ornaments, sacred metal for sacred uses. Even butter-lamps are made of gold. Unfortunately, the metal is so soft that ornaments are easily distorted.

Tibet is about eight times the size of the British Isles. Large areas are practically unexplored, but from my own travels with the Lama Mingyar Dondup I know there is gold, silver, and uranium. We have never permitted Western peoples to survey—in spite of their fevered attempts!—because of the old legend: "Where the Men of the West go, there goes war!" It should be remembered, when reading of "gold trumpets", "gold dishes", "gold-covered bodies", that gold is *not* a rare metal in Tibet, but a sacred one. Tibet could be one of the great storehouses of the world if mankind would work together in peace instead of so much useless striving for power.

One morning the Lama Mingyar Dondup came in to me where I was copying an old manuscript ready for the carvers.

"Lobsang, you will have to leave that for now. The Precious One has sent for us. We have to go to Norbu Linga and together, unseen, we have to analyse the colours of some foreigner from the Western world. You *must* hurry to get ready, the Precious One wants to see us first. No scarves, no ceremony, only speed!"

So that was that. I gaped at him for a moment, then jumped to my feet. "A clean robe, Honourable Lama Master, and I am ready."

It did not take me long to make myself look passably tidy. Together we set off down the hill on foot, the distance was about half a mile. At the bottom of the mountain, just by the spot where I had fallen and broken my bones, we went over a little bridge and reached the Lingkhor road. This we crossed, and reached the gate of the Norbu Linga, or Jewel Park, as it is sometimes translated. The guards were just about to warn us off when they saw that the Lama Mingyar Dondup was with me. Then their attitudes changed completely; we were quickly shown into the Inner Garden where the Dalai Lama was sitting on a veranda. I felt a little foolish, having no scarf to present, and not knowing how to behave without it. The Inmost One looked up with a smile: "Oh! Sit down, Mingyar, and you, too, Lobsang. You have certainly hurried."

We sat down and waited for him to speak. He meditated for some time, seeming to marshal his thoughts in an orderly array.

"Some time ago," he said, "the army of the Red Barbarians (the British) invaded our sacred land. I went to India and from thence travelled most extensively. In the Year of the Iron Dog (1910) the Chinese invaded us as a direct result of the British invasion. I again went to India and there I met the man whom we are to meet today. I say all this for you, Lobsang, for Mingyar was with me. The British made promises and they were not kept. Now I want to know if this man speaks with one or two tongues. You, Lobsang, will not understand his speech and so will not be influenced by it. From this lattice screen you and another will watch unobserved, your presence will not be known. You will write down your astral-colour impressions as taught by our Guide, who speaks so well of you. Now show him to his place, Mingyar, for he is more used to you than to me and—I do believe—he considers the Lama Mingyar Dondup to be superior to the Dalai Lama!"

Behind the lattice screen I had grown tired of looking about. Tired of watching the birds and the waving of the branches of the trees. Now and then I took surreptitious nibbles at some tsampa which I had with me. Clouds drifted across the sky, and I thought how nice it would be to feel the sway and tremor of a kite beneath me, with the rushing wind whistling through the fabric and thrumming on the rope. Suddenly I jumped as there was a crash. For a moment I thought that I *was* in a kite, and had fallen asleep and out! But no, the gate to the Inner Garden had been flung open, and golden-robed lamas of the Household escorted in a most extraordinary sight. I was hard put to keep silent; I wanted to explode with laughter. A man, a tall, thin man. White hair, white face, scanty eyebrows, and deep-sunk eyes. Quite a hard mouth. But his *dress*! Blue cloth of some sort with a whole row of knobs down the front, shiny knobs. Apparently some very bad tailor had made the clothes, for the collar was so big that it had to be folded over. It was folded over certain patches on the sides, too. I thought that the Westerners must have some symbolic patches such as those we used in imitation of Buddha. Pockets meant nothing to me in those days, nor did folded collars. In Tibet, those who have no need to do manual work have long sleeves which completely hide the hands. This man had short sleeves, reaching only to his wrists. "Yet he cannot be a labourer," I thought, "for

154

his hands look too soft. Perhaps he does not know *how* to dress."
But this fellow's robe ended where his legs joined his body. "Poor,
very poor," I thought. His trousers were too tight in the leg and
too long, for the bottoms were *turned up*. "He must feel terrible,
looking like that in front of the Inmost One," I thought. "I wonder
if someone his size will lend him proper clothes." Then I looked at
his feet. Very, very strange. He had some curious black things on
them. Shiny things, shiny as if they were covered with ice. Not
boots of felt such as we wear, no, I decided that I would never see
anything stranger than this. Quite automatically I was writing
down the colours, I saw, and making notes of my own interpreta-
tion of them. Sometimes the man spoke in Tibetan, quite good for
a foreigner, then lapsed into the most remarkable collection of
sounds I had ever heard. "English", as they told me afterwards
when I again saw the Dalai Lama.

The man amazed me by reaching into one of the patches at his
side and bringing out a piece of white cloth. Before my astounded
eyes he put this cloth over his mouth and nose and made it sound
like a small trumpet. "Some sort of a salute to the Precious One,"
I thought. Salute over, he carefully put away the cloth behind the
same patch. He fiddled about with other patches and brought out
various papers of a type I had not seen before. White, thin, smooth
paper. Not like ours which was buff, thick, and rough. "How can
one possibly write on that?" I thought. "There is nothing to
scrape away the crayon, things would just slide off!" The man
took from behind one of his patches a thin stick of painted wood
with what looked like soot in the middle. With this he made the
strangest squiggles I had ever imagined. I thought he could not
write and was just pretending to by making these markings.
"Soot? Who ever heard of anyone writing with a streak of soot.
Just let him blow on it and see the soot fly off!"

He was obviously a cripple because he had to sit on a wooden
framework which rested on four sticks. He sat down on the frame,
and let his legs hang over the edge. I thought that his spine must
have been damaged, because two more sticks from the frame on
which he sat supported it. By now I was feeling really sorry for
him: ill-fitting clothes, inability to write, showing off by blowing
a trumpet from his pocket, and now, to make it even stranger, he
could not sit properly but had to have his back supported and his
legs dangling. He fidgeted a lot, crossing and uncrossing his legs.
At one time, to my horror, he tipped the left foot so that the sole
was pointing at the Dalai Lama, a terrible insult if done by a
Tibetan, but he soon remembered and uncrossed his legs again.
The Inmost One did great honour to this man, for he also sat on

one of these wooden frames and let his legs hang over. The visitor had a most peculiar name, he was called "Female Musical Instrument", and he had two decorations in front of it. Now I should refer to him as "C. A. Bell". By his auric colours I judged him to be in poor health, most probably caused by living in a climate to which he was not suited. He appeared genuine in his desire to be helpful, but it was obvious from his colours that he was afraid of annoying his government and of having his after-work pension affected. *He* wanted to take one course, but his government was not willing, so he had to say one thing and hope that his opinions and suggestions would be proved correct by time.

We knew a lot about this Mr. Bell. We had all the data, his birth time, and various "highlights" in his career with which one could plot his course of events. The astrologers discovered that he had previously lived in Tibet and had, during his last life, expressed the wish to reincarnate in the West in the hope of assisting in an understanding between East and West. I have recently been given to understand that he mentions this in some book that he has written. Certainly we felt that if he had been able to influence his government in the way he desired there would have been no Communist invasion of my country. However, the forecasts decreed that there would be such an invasion, and the predictions are never wrong.

The English Government seemed to be very suspicious: they thought that Tibet was making treaties with Russia. This did not suit them. England would not make a treaty with Tibet, nor was she willing for Tibet to make friends with anyone else. Sikkin, Bhutan, anywhere but Tibet could have treaties, but not Tibet. So the English became hot under their peculiar collars in an attempt to invade us or strangle us—they did not mind which. This Mr. Bell, who was on the spot, saw that we had no desire to side with any nation; we wanted to stay on our own, to live life in our own way, and keep clear of all dealings with foreigners who, in the past, had brought us nothing but trouble, loss, and hardship.

The Inmost One was pleased indeed with my remarks after this Mr. Bell had left. But he thought of me in terms of more work! "Yes, yes!" he exclaimed, "we must develop you even more, Lobsang. You will find it of the utmost use when you go to the Far Countries. We will have you given more hypnotic treatment, we must cram in all the knowledge that we can." He reached for his bell and rang for one of his attendants. "Mingyar Dondup, I want him here, *now*!" he said. A few minutes later my Guide appeared and made his leisurely way across. Not for anyone would that Lama hurry! And the Dalai Lama knew him as a friend and so did not try to hasten him. My Guide sat beside me, in front of the Precious One. An attendant hurried along with more buttered tea and "things from India" to eat. When we were settled, the Dalai Lama said: "Mingyar, you were correct, he *has* ability. He can be developed still more, Mingyar, and he *must* be. Take whatever steps you consider necessary so that he is trained as quickly and as thoroughly as possible. Use any and all of our resources for, as we have been so often warned, evil times will come upon our country, and we must have someone who can compile the Record of the Ancient Arts."

So the tempo of my days were increased. Often, from this time, I was sent for in a hurry to "interpret" the colours of some person, perhaps that of a learned abbot from a far distant lamasery, or a civil leader of some remote province. I became a well-known visitor to the Potala and to the Norbu Linga. In the former I was able to make use of the telescopes which I so enjoyed, particularly one large astronomical model on a heavy tripod. With this, late at night, I would spend hours watching the moon and the stars.

The Lama Mingyar Dondup and I frequently went into Lhasa City to observe visitors. His own considerable powers of clairvoyance, and his wide knowledge of people, enabled him to check and develop my own statements. It was most interesting to go to the stall of a trader and hear the man speak loud in praise of his wares, and compare them with his thoughts, which to us were not so private. My memory, too, was developed, for long hours I listened to involved passages, and then had to say them back. For unknown periods of time I lay in a hypnotic trance while people read to me passages from our oldest Scriptures.

CHAPTER FIFTEEN

THE SECRET NORTH—AND YETIS

DURING this time we went to the Chang Tang Highlands. In this book there is no time for more than a brief mention of this region. To do the expedition justice would require several books. The Dala Lama had blessed each of the fifteen members of the party and we had all set off in high spirits, mounted on mules: mules will go where horses will not. We made our slow way along by Tengri Tso, on to the huge lakes at Zilling Nor, and ever northwards. The slow climb over the Tangla Range, and on into unexplored territory. It is difficult to say how long we took, because time meant nothing to us: there was no reason for us to hurry, we went at our own comfortable speed and saved our strength and energy for later exertions.

As we made our way farther and farther into the Highlands, the ground ever rising, I was reminded of the face of the moon as seen through the large telescope at the Potala. Immense mountain ranges, and deep canyons. Here the vista was the same. The unending, eternal mountains, and crevices which seemed bottomless. We struggled on through this "lunar landscape", finding the conditions becoming harder and harder. At last the mules could go no farther. In the rarefied air they were soon spent and could not manage to cross some of the rocky gorges where we swung dizzily at the end of a yak-hair rope. In the most sheltered spot we could find we left our mules and the five weakest members of the party stayed with them. They were sheltered from the worst blasts of that barren, wind-swept landscape by a spur of rock which towered upwards like a jagged wolf-fang. At the base there was a cave where softer rock had been eroded by time. A precipitous path could be followed which would lead downwards to a valley where there was sparse vegetation on which the mules could feed.

A tinkling stream dashed along the tableland and rushed over the edge of a cliff to fall thousands of feet below, so far below that even the sound of its landing was lost.

Here we rested for two days before plodding on higher and higher. Our backs ached with the loads we were carrying, and our lungs felt as if they would burst for want of air. On we went, over crevices and ravines. Over many of them we had to toss iron hooks to which ropes were attached. Toss, and hope that there would be a safe hold at the other side. We would take turns to swing the rope with the hook, and take turns to swarm across when a hold was secured. Once across we had another end of rope so that when all the party had negotiated the canyon, the rope also could be brought over by pulling one end. Sometimes we could get no hold. Then one of us would have the rope tied around his waist, and from the highest point we could reach, would try to swing like a pendulum, increasing the momentum with each swing. With one of us across the other side, he would have to clamber up as best he could in order to reach a point where the rope would be roughly horizontal. We all took it in turns to do this, as it was hard and dangerous work. One monk was killed doing it. He had climbed high on our side of a cliff and let himself swing. Apparently he badly misjudged, for he crashed into the opposite wall with terrible force, leaving his face and his brains on the points of the jagged rocks. We hauled the body back, and had a service for him. There was no way of burying the body in solid rock, so we left him for the wind and the rain and the birds. The monk whose turn it now was did not look at all happy, so I went instead. It was obvious to me that in view of the predictions about me, I should be quite safe, and my faith was rewarded. My own swing was cautious—in spite of the prediction!—and I reached with scrabbling fingers for the edge of the nearest rock. Only just did I manage to hang on and pull myself up, with the breath rasping my throat, and my heart pounding as if it would explode. For a time I lay, quite spent, then I managed to crawl a painful way up the mountain-side. The others, the best companions that anyone could have, swung their other rope to give me the best possible chance of reaching it. With the two ends now in my grasp, I made them secure and called out to them to pull hard and test it. One by one they came over, upside down, hands and feet linked over the rope, robes fluttering in the still breeze, the breeze which impeded us and did not help our breathing at all.

At the top of the cliff we rested a while and made our tea, although at this altitude the boiling-point was low, and the tea did not really warm us. Somewhat less tired now, we again took up our loads and stumbled onwards into the heart of this terrible region. Soon we came to a sheet of ice, a glacier, maybe, and our progress became even more difficult. We had no spiked boots, no ice-axes, or mountaineering equipment; our only "equipment" consisted of our ordinary felt boots with the soles bound with hair to afford some grip, and ropes.

In passing, Tibetan mythology has a Cold Hell. Warmth is a blessing to us, so the opposite is cold, hence the cold hell. This trip to the Highlands showed me what cold could be!

After three days of this shuffling upwards over the ice-sheet, shivering in the bitter wind and wishing that we had never seen the place, the glacier led us downwards between towering rocks. Down and down we went, fumbling and slipping, down into an unknown depth. Several miles farther on we rounded a shoulder of a mountain and saw before us a dense white fog. From a distance we did not know if it was snow or cloud, it was so white and un-broken. As we approached we saw that it was indeed fog, as tendrils kept breaking away and drifting off.

The Lama Mingyar Dondup, the only one of us who had been here before, smiled with satisfaction: "You *do* look a cheerless lot! But you will have some pleasure now."

We saw nothing pleasant before us. Fog. Cold. Frozen ice below our feet and frozen sky above our heads. Jagged rocks like the fangs in a wolf's mouth, rocks against which we bruised ourselves. And my Guide said that we were going to have "some pleasure"!

On into the cold and clammy fog we went, miserably plodding we knew not where. Hugging our robes about us for an illusion of warmth. Panting and shuddering with the cold. Farther, and yet farther in. And stopped, petrified with amazement and fright. The fog was becoming *warm*, the ground was growing *hot*. Those behind who had not reached so far, and could not see, bumped into us. Recovered somewhat from our stupefaction by the Lama Mingyar Dondup's laughter, we pushed forward again, blindly, reaching out for the man ahead, the one in the lead feeling un-seeingly with his out-thrust staff. Below our feet stones threatened to trip us, pebbles rolled beneath our boots. Stones? Pebbles? Then where was the glacier, the ice? Quite suddenly the fog thinned, and we were through it. One by one we fumbled our way into—well, as I looked about me I thought that I had died of cold and had been transported to the Heavenly Fields. I rubbed my eyes with hot hands; I pinched myself and rapped my knuckles against a rock to see if I was flesh or spirit. But then I looked about: my eight companions were with me. Could we *all* have been so suddenly transported? And if so, what about the tenth member who had been killed against the rock face? And were we *all* worthy of the heaven I saw before us?

Thirty heart-beats before we had been shivering with cold the other side of the fog-curtain. Now we were on the edge of collapse with the heat! The air shimmered, the ground steamed. A stream at our feet bubbled out of the earth itself, propelled by gouts of steam. About us there was green grass, greener than any I had ever seen before. Broad-leaved grass stood before us more than knee-high. We were dazed and frightened. Here was magic, something quite beyond our experience. Then the Lama Mingyar Dondup spoke: "If I looked like that when I first saw it, then I *did* look a sight! You fellows look as if you think the Ice Gods are having a sport with you."

We looked about, almost too frightened to move, and then my Guide spoke again: "Let us jump over the stream, *jump* over, for the water is boiling. A few miles farther and we shall reach a really beautiful spot where we can rest."

He was right, as ever. About three miles on we lay at full length on the moss-covered ground, lay without our robes as we felt as if we were being boiled. Here there were trees such as I had never seen before, and probably never shall see again. Highly coloured flowers bestrewed everything. Climbing vines laced the tree trunks and depended from the branches. Slightly to the right of the pleasant glade in which we rested we could see a small lake and ripples and circles on its surface indicated the presence of life within it. We still felt bewitched, we were sure that we had been overcome with the heat and passed to another plane of existence. Or had we been overcome with the cold? We did not know!

The foliage was luxuriant, now that I have travelled I should say that it was tropical. There were birds of a type even now strange to me. This was volcanic territory. Hot springs bubbled from the ground, and there were sulphurous odours. My Guide told us that there were, to his knowledge, two places only like this in the Highlands. He said that the underground heat, and the hot streams, melted the ice, and the high rock walls of the valley trapped the warm air. The dense white fog we had penetrated was the meeting-place of the hot and cold streams. He also told us that he had seen giant animal skeletons, skeletons which, in life, must have supported an animal twenty or thirty feet high. Later I saw such bones myself.

Here I had my first sight of a yeti. I was bending picking herbs, when something made me look up. There, within ten yards of me, was this creature that I had heard so much about. Parents in Tibet often threaten naughty children with: "Behave yourself, or a yeti will get you!" Now, I thought, a yeti *had* got me. And I was not happy about it. We looked at each other, both of us frozen with fright for a period which seemed ageless. It was pointing a hand at me, and uttering a curious mewing noise like a kitten. The head seemed to have no frontal lobes, but sloped back almost directly from the very heavy brows. The chin receded greatly and the teeth were large and prominent. Yet the skull capacity appeared similar to that of modern man with the exception of the missing forehead. The hands and feet were large and splayed. The legs were bowed and the arms were much longer than normal. I observed that the creature walked on the outer side of the feet as humans do. (Apes and others of that order do not walk on the outer surfaces.)

As I looked and perhaps jumped with fright, or from some other cause, the yeti screeched, turned, and leaped away. It seemed to make "one-leg" jumps and the result was like giant strides. My own reaction was also to run, in the opposite direction! Later, thinking about it, I came to the conclusion that I must have broken the Tibetan sprint record for altitudes above seventeen thousand feet.

Later we saw a few yetis in the distance. They hastened to hide at sight of us, and we certainly did not provoke them. The Lama Mingyar Dondup told us that these yetis were throwbacks of the human race who had taken a different path in evolution and who could only live in the most secluded places. Quite frequently we heard tales of yetis who had left the Highlands and had been seen leaping and bounding near inhabited regions. There are tales of lone women who have been carried off by male yetis. That may be one way in which they continue their line. Certainly some nuns confirmed this for us later when they told us that one of their Order had been carried off by a yeti in the night. However, on such things I am not competent to write. I can only say that I have seen yetis and baby yetis. I have also seen skeletons of them.

Some people have expressed doubts about the truth of my statements concerning the yetis. People have apparently written books of guesses about them, but none of these authors have *seen* one, as they admit. I have. A few years ago Marconi was laughed at when he said he was going to send a message by radio across the Atlantic. Western doctors solemnly asserted that Man could not travel at more than fifty miles an hour or they would die through the rush of air. There have been tales about a fish which was said to be a "living fossil". Now scientists have seen them, captured them, dissected them. And if Western Man had his way, our poor old yetis would be captured, dissected, and preserved in spirit. We believe that yetis have been driven to the Highlands and that elsewhere, except for very infrequent wanderers, they are extinct. The first sight of one causes fright. The second time one is filled with compassion for these creatures of a bygone age who are doomed to extinction through the strains of modern life.

I am prepared, when the Communists are chased out of Tibet, to accompany an expedition of sceptics and *show* them the yetis in the Highlands. It will be worth it to see the faces of these big business men when confronted with something beyond their commercial experience. They can use oxygen and bearers, I will use my old monk's robe. Cameras will prove the truth. We had no photographic equipment in Tibet in those days.

Our old legends relate that centuries ago Tibet had shores washed by the seas. Certain it is that fossils of fish and other marine creatures are to be found if the surface of the earth is disturbed. The Chinese have a similar belief. The Tablet of Yü which formerly stood on the Kou-lou peak of Mount Hêng in the province of Hu-pei records that the Great Yü rested upon the site (in 2278 B.C.) after his labour of draining off the "waters of the deluge" which at the time submerged all China except the highest lands. The original stone has, I believe, been removed, but there are imitations at Wu-ch'ang Fu, a place near Hankow. A further copy is in the Yu-lin temple near Shao-hsing Fu in Chekiang. According to our belief, Tibet was once a low land, by the sea, and for reasons beyond our certain knowledge there were frightful earth-convulsions during which many lands sank beneath the waters, and others rose up as mountains.

The Chang Tang Highlands were rich in fossils, and in evidence that all this area had been a seashore. Giant shells, of vivid colours, curious stone sponges, and ridges of coral were common. Gold, too, was here, lumps of it which could be picked up as easily as could the pebbles. The waters which flowed from the depths of the earth were of all temperatures from boiling gouts of steam to near-freezing. It was a land of fantastic contrasts. Here there was a hot, humid atmosphere such as we had never before experienced. A few yards away, just the other side of a fog-curtain, there was the bitter cold that could sap the life and render a body as brittle as glass. The rarest of rare herbs grew here, and for those alone we had made this journey. Fruits were there, too, fruits such as we had never before seen. We tasted them, liked them, and satiated ourselves . . . the penalty was a hard one. During the night and the whole of next day we were too busy to gather herbs. Our stomachs were not used to such food. We left those fruits alone after that!

We loaded ourselves to the limit with herbs and plants, and retraced our footsteps through the fog. The cold the other side was terrible. Probably all of us felt like turning back and living in the luxuriant valley. One lama was unable to face the cold again. A few hours after passing the fog-curtain he collapsed, and although we camped then in an effort to help him, he was beyond aid, and went to the Heavenly Fields during the night. We did our best—throughout that night we had tried to warm him, lying on each side of him, but the bitter cold of that arid region was too much. He slept, and did not awaken. His load we shared between us, although we had considered before that we were laden to the limit. Back over that glittering sheet of age-old ice we retraced our painful steps. Our strength seemed to have been sapped by the comfortable warmth of the hidden valley, and we had insufficient food now. For the last two days of our journey back to the mules we did not eat at all—we had nothing left, not even tea.

With yet a few more miles to go, one of the men in the lead toppled over, and did not rise. Cold, hunger, and hardship had taken one more from among us. And there was still another who had departed. We arrived at the base camp to find four monks waiting for us. Four monks who leapt to their feet to aid us cover the last few yards to this stage. Four. The fifth had ventured out in a gale of wind and had been blown over the edge into the canyon below. By laying face down, and having my feet held so that I could not slip, I saw him lying hundreds of feet below, covered in his blood red robe which was now, literally, blood red.

During the next three days we rested and tried to regain some of our strength. It was not merely tiredness and exhaustion which prevented us from moving, but the wind which shrilled among the rocks, trundling pebbles before it, sending cutting blasts of dust-laden air into our cave. The surface of the little stream was whipped off and blown away like a fine spray. Through the night the gale howled around us like ravening demons lusting for our flesh. From somewhere near came a rushing, and a "crump-crump" followed by an earth-shaking thud. Yet another immense boulder from the mountain ranges had succumbed to the attrition of wind and water and caused a landslide. Early in the morning of the second day, before the first light had reached the valley below, while we were still in the pre-dawn luminescence of the mountains, a huge boulder crashed from the peak above us. We heard it coming and huddled together, making ourselves as small as possible. Down it crashed, as if the Devils were driving their chariots at us from the skies. Down it roared, accompanied by a shower of stones. A horrid crash and trembling as it struck the rocky table-land in front of us. The edge shook and wavered, and some ten or twelve feet of the ledge toppled and broke away. From below, quite a time later, came the echo and reverberation of the falling debris. So was our comrade buried.

The weather seemed to be getting worse. We decided that we would leave early on the next morning before we were prevented. Our equipment—such as it was—was carefully overhauled. Ropes were tested, and the mules examined for any sores or cuts. At dawn of the next day the weather seemed to be a little calmer. We left with feelings of pleasure at the thought of being homeward bound. Now we were a party of eleven instead of the fifteen who had so cheerfully started out. Day after day we plodded on, footsore and weary, our mules bearing their loads of herbs. Our progress was slow. Time had no meaning for us. We toiled on in a daze of fatigue. Now we were on half-rations, and constantly hungry.

At last we came in sight of the lakes again, and to our great joy we saw that a caravan of yaks grazed near by. The traders welcomed us, pressed food and tea on us and did all they could to ease our weariness. We were tattered and bruised. Our robes were in rags, and our feet were bleeding where great blisters had burst. But—we had been to the Chang Tang Highlands and returned— some of us! My Guide had now been twice, perhaps the only man in the world to have made *two* such journeys.

The traders looked after us well. Crouched round the yak-dung fire in the dark of the night they wagged their heads in amazement as we told of our experiences. We enjoyed *their* tales of journeys to India, and of meetings with other traders from the Hindu Kush. We were sorry to leave these men and wished that they were going in our direction. They had but recently set out from Lhasa; we were returning there. So, in the morning, we parted with mutual expressions of good will.

Many monks will not converse with traders, but the Lama Mingyar Dondup taught that all men are equal: race, colour, or creed meant naught. It was a man's intentions and actions only that counted.

Now our strength was renewed, we were going *home*. The countryside became greener, more fertile, and at last we came in sight of the gleaming gold of the Potala and our own Chakpori, just a little higher than the Peak. Mules are wise animals—ours were in a hurry to get to their own home in Shö, and they pulled so hard that we had difficulty in restraining them. One would have thought that *they* had been to the Chang Tang—and not us!

We climbed the stony road up the Iron Mountain with joy. Joy at being back from Chambala, as we call the frozen north.

Now began our round of receptions, but first we had to see the Inmost One. His reaction was illuminating. "You have done what

I should like to do, seen what I ardently desire to see. Here I have 'all-power', yet I am a prisoner of my people. The greater the power, the less the freedom: the higher the rank, the more a servant. And I would give it all to see what you have seen."

The Lama Mingyar Dondup, as leader of the expedition, was given the Scarf of Honour, with the red triple knots. I, because I was the youngest member, was similarly honoured. I well knew that an award at "both ends" embraced everything in between!

For weeks after we were travelling to other lamaseries, to lecture, to distribute special herbs, and to give *me* the opportunity of seeing other districts. First we had to visit "The Three Seats", Drepung, Sera, and Ganden. From thence we went farther afield, to Dorje-thag, and to Samye, both on the River Tsangpo, forty miles away. We also visited Samden Lamasery, between the Dü-me and Yamdok Lakes, fourteen thousand feet above sea-level. It was a relief to follow the course of our own river, the Kyi Chu. For us it was truly well named, the River of Happiness.

All the time my instruction had been continued while we rode, when we stopped, and when we rested. Now the time of my examination for the Lama degree was near, and so we returned once again to Chakpori in order that I should not be distracted.

ༀམཎིཔདྨེཧཱུྃ

CHAPTER SIXTEEN

LAMAHOOD

A CONSIDERABLE amount of training was now given to me in the art of astral travelling, where the spirit, or ego, leaves the body and remains connected to life on Earth only by the Silver Cord. Many people find it difficult to believe that we travel in this way. *Everyone* does, when they sleep. Nearly always in the West it is involuntary; in the East lamas can do it when fully conscious. Thus they have a complete *memory* of what they have done, what they have seen and where they have been. In the West people have lost the art, and so when they return to wakefulness they think they have had a "dream".

All countries had a knowledge of this astral journeying. In England it is alleged that "witches can fly". Broomsticks are not necessary, except as a means of rationalizing what people do not *want* to believe! In the U.S.A. the "Spirits of the Red Men" are said to fly. In all countries, everywhere, there is a buried knowledge of such things. I was taught to do it. So can anyone be.

Telepathy is another art which is easy to master. But not if it is going to be used as a stage turn. Fortunately this art is now gaining some recognition. Hypnotism is yet another art of the East. I have carried out major operations on hypnotized patients, such as leg amputations and those of an equally serious nature. The patient feels nothing, suffers nothing, and awakens in better condition through not having to also suffer the effects of the orthodox anaesthetics. Now, so I am told, hypnotism is being used to a limited extent in England.

Invisibility is another matter. It is a very good thing that invisibility is beyond more than the very, very few. The principle is easy: the practice is difficult. Think of what attracts you. A noise? A quick movement or a flashing colour? Noises and quick actions rouse people, make them notice one. An immobile person is not so easily seen, nor is a "familiar" type or class of person. The man who brings the mail, often people will say that "no one has been here, no one at all", yet their mail will have been brought. How, by an invisible man? Or one who is such a familiar sight that he is not "seen", or perceived. (A policeman is always seen as nearly everyone has a guilty conscience!) To attain a state of invisibility one must suspend action, and *also suspend one's brain waves!* If the physical brain is allowed to function (think), any other person near by becomes telepathically aware (sees) and so the state of invisibility is lost. There are men in Tibet who can become invisible at will, but they are able to shield their brain waves. It is perhaps fortunate that they are so few in number.

Levitation *can* be accomplished, and sometimes is, solely for the technical exercise involved. It is a clumsy method of moving around. The effort involved is considerable. The real adept uses astral travelling, which is truly a matter of the utmost simplicity . . . provided one has a good teacher. I had, and I could (and can) do astral travelling. I could *not* make myself invisible, in spite of my most earnest efforts. It would have been a great blessing to be able to vanish when I was wanted to do something unpleasant, but this was denied me. Nor, as I have said before, was I possessed of musical talents. My singing voice brought down the wrath of the Music Master, but that wrath was as naught to the commotion I caused when I tried to play the cymbals—thinking that *anyone* could use *those* things—and quite accidentally caught a poor unfortunate monk on each side of his head. I was advised, unkindly, to stick to clairvoyance and medicine!

We did much of what is termed yoga in the Western world. It is, of course, a very great science and one which can improve a human almost beyond belief. My own personal opinion is that yoga is not suitable for Western people without very considerable modification. The science has been known to us for centuries; we are taught the postures from the very earliest age. Our limbs, skeleton, and muscles are trained to yoga. Western people, perhaps of middle age, who try some of these postures can definitely harm themselves. It is merely my opinion as a Tibetan, but I do feel that unless there is a set of exercises which have been so modified, people should be warned against trying them. Again, one needs a very good native teacher, one thoroughly trained in male and female anatomy if harm is to be avoided. Not merely the postures can do harm, but the breathing exercises also!

Breathing to a particular pattern is the main secret of many Tibetan phenomena. But here again, unless one has a wise and experienced teacher, such exercises can be extremely harmful, if not fatal. Many travellers have written of "the racing ones", lamas who can control the weight of the body (*not* levitation) and race at high speed for hours and hours over the ground, hardly touching the earth in passing. It takes much practice, and the "racer" has to be in a semi-trance state. Evening is the best time, when there are stars upon which to gaze, and the terrain must be monotonous, with nothing to break the semi-trance state. The man who is speeding so is in a condition similar to that of a sleep-walker. He visualizes his destination, keeps it constantly before his Third Eye, and unceasingly recites the appropriate mantra. Hour after hour he will race, and reach his destination untired. This system has only one advantage over astral travelling. When travelling by the latter, one moves in the spirit state and so cannot move material objects, cannot, for example, carry one's belongings. The arjopa, as one calls the "racer", can carry his normal load, but he labours under disadvantages in his turn.

Correct breathing enables Tibetan adepts to sit naked on ice, seventeen thousand feet or so above sea-level, and keep hot, so hot that the ice is melted and the adept freely perspires.

A digression for a moment: the other day I said that I had done this myself at eighteen thousand feet above sea-level. My listener, quite seriously, asked me: "With the tide in, or out?"

Have you ever tried to lift a heavy object when your lungs were empty of air? Try it and you will discover it to be almost impossible. Then fill your lungs as much as you can, hold your breath, and lift with ease. Or you may be frightened, or angry, take a deep breath, as deep as you can, and hold it for ten seconds. Then exhale slowly. Repeat three times at least and you will find that your heart-beats are slowed up and you feel calm. These are things which can be tried by anyone at all without harm. A knowledge of breath control helped me to withstand Japanese tortures and more tortures when I was a prisoner of the Communists. The Japanese at their worst are *gentlemen* compared to the Communists! I know both, at their worst.

The time had now come when I was to take the actual examination for lamahood. Before this I had to be blessed by the Dalai Lama. Every year he blesses every monk in Tibet, individually, not in bulk as does, for example, the Pope of Rome. The Inmost One touches the majority with a tassel attached to a stick. Those whom he favours, or who are of high rank, he touches on the head with one hand. The highly favoured are blessed by him placing two hands on the person's head. For the first time he placed both hands on me and said in a low voice: "You are doing well, my boy: do even better at your examination. Justify the faith we have placed in you."

Three days before my sixteenth birthday I presented myself for examination together with about fourteen other candidates. The "examination boxes" seemed to be smaller, or perhaps it was that I was bigger. When I lay on the floor, with my feet against one wall, I could touch the other wall with my hands above my head, but my arms had to be bent as there was not enough room to stretch them straight. The boxes were square, and at the front the wall was such that I could just touch the top with my outstretched hands, again with my arms above my head. The back wall was about twice my height. There was no roof, so at least we had ample air! Once again we were searched before entering, and all we were allowed to take in were our wooden bowl, our rosary, and writing material. With the Invigilators satisfied, we were led one by one to a box, told to enter, and after we had done so the door was shut and a bar put across. Then the Abbot and the Head Examiner came and fixed a huge seal, so that the door could not be opened. A trap-hatch some seven inches square could be opened only from the outside. Through this we were passed examination papers at the beginning of each day. The worked papers were collected at dusk. Tsampa was passed in as well, once a day. Buttered tea was different, we could have as much as we wanted by merely calling "pö-cha kesho" (bring tea). As we were not allowed out for any purpose whatever, we did not drink too much!

My own stay in that box was for ten days. I was taking the herbal examination, anatomy, a subject of which I had already a very good knowledge, and divinity. Those subjects occupied me from first to last light for five seemingly endless days. The sixth day brought a change, and a commotion. From a nearby box came howls and screams. Running footsteps, and a babble of voices. Clatter of a heavy wooden door being unbarred. Soothing murmurs, and the screams subsided to a sobbing undertone. For one, the examination had ended. For me, the second half was about to start. An hour late, the sixth day's papers were brought. Metaphysics. Yoga. Nine branches of it. And I had to pass in the whole lot.

Five branches are known very slightly to the Western world: Hatha yoga teaches mastery over the purely physical body, or "vehicle", as we term it. Kundalini yoga gives one psychic power, clairvoyance, and similar powers. Laya yoga teaches mastery over the mind, one of its offshoots is to remember permanently a thing once read or heard. Raja yoga prepares one for transcendental consciousness and wisdom. Samadhi yoga leads to supreme illumination and enables one to glimpse the purpose and plan beyond life on Earth. This is the branch which enables one, at the instant of leaving this earth-life, to grasp the Greater Reality and abandon the Round of Rebirth; unless one decided to return to

Earth for a special purpose, such as to help others in some particular way. The other forms of yoga cannot be discussed in a book of this nature, and certainly my knowledge of the English language is inadequate to do justice to such illustrious subjects.

So, for another five days I was busy, like a broody hen in a box. But even ten-day-long examinations have to end, and as the lama collected the last papers on the tenth night, he was greeted with smiles of delight. That night we had vegetables with our tsampa, the very first change from this one basic food for ten days at least. That night it was easy to sleep. At no time had I worried about passing, but I did worry about the degree of pass; I had been commanded to be high on the final list. In the morning the seals were broken from the doors, the bars were lifted, and we had to clean our examination boxes before being able to leave. For a week we were able to recover our strength after the considerable ordeal. Then came two days of judo in which we tried all our holds, and made each other unconscious with our "anaesthetic holds". Two days more were devoted to an oral examination on the written papers, in which the examiners questioned us about our weak points only. Let me emphasize that each candidate was orally examined for two whole days *each*. Another week, during which we reacted according to our temperaments, and then the results were announced. To my noisily expressed joy, I was again at the top of the list. My joy was for two reasons: it proved that the Lama Mingyar Dondup was the best teacher of all, and I knew that the Dalai Lama would be pleased with my teacher and with me.

Some days later, when the Lama Mingyar Dondup was instructing me in his room, the door was thrust open, and a panting messenger, tongue lolling and eyes staring, burst in upon us. In his hands he bore the cleft stick of messages. "From the Inmost One," he gasped, "to the Honourable Medical Lama Tuesday Lobsang Rampa". With that he took from his robe the letter, wrapped in the silken scarf of greeting. "With all speed, Honourable Sir, I have rushed here." Relieved of his burden, he turned and dashed out even faster—in search of chang!

That message: no, I was not going to open it. Certainly it was addressed to me, but . . . what was in it? More studies? More work? It looked very large, and very official. So long as I had not opened it I could not know what was inside, so could not be blamed for not doing this or that. Or so my first thoughts went. My Guide was sitting back laughing at me, so I passed the letter, scarf and all, to him. He took it and opened the envelope, or outer wrapping. Two folded sheets were inside, these he spread open and read, deliberately being slow about it to tease me further. At last, when I was in a fever of impatience to know the worst, he said: "It is all right, you can breathe again. We have to go to the Potala to see him without delay. That means *now*, Lobsang. It says here that I have to go as well." He touched the gong at his side, and to the attendant who entered, he gave instructions that our two white horses be saddled immediately. Quickly we changed our robes and selected our two best white scarves. Together we went to the Abbot and told him that we had to go to the Potala to see the Inmost One. "The Peak, eh? He was at the Norbu Linga yesterday. Oh well, you have the letter to say which it is. It must be very official."

In the courtyard monk grooms were waiting with our horses. We mounted and clattered down the mountain-path. Just a little way farther on, and we had to climb up the other mountain, the Potala, really it was hardly worth the fuss of trying to sit on a horse! The one advantage was that the horses would carry us up the steps almost to the top of the Peak. Attendants were waiting for us, as soon as we had dismounted, our horses were led away, and we were hurried off to the Inmost One's private quarters. I entered alone and made my prostrations and scarf presentation.

"Sit down, Lobsang," he said, "I am very pleased with you. I am very pleased with Mingyar for his part in your success. I have read all your examination papers myself."

That caused a shiver of fright. One of my many failings, so I have been told, is that I have a somewhat misplaced sense of humour. Sometimes it had broken out in answering the examination questions, because some questions simply invite that sort of answer! The Dalai Lama read my thoughts, for he laughed outright and said, "Yes, you have a sense of humour at the wrong times, but . . ." a long pause, during which I feared the worst, then, "I enjoyed every word."

For two hours I was with him. During the second hour my Guide was sent for and the Inmost One gave instructions concerning my further training. I was to undergo the Ceremony of the Little Death, I was to visit—with the Lama Mingyar Dondup—other lamaseries, and I was to study with the Breakers of the Dead. As these latter were of low caste, and their work of such a nature, the Dalai Lama gave me a written script in order that I could keep my own status. He called upon the Body Breakers to render me "all and every assistance in order that the secrets of the bodies may be laid bare and so that the physical reason for the body being discarded may be discovered. He is also to take possession of any body or parts of a body that he may require for his studies." So that was that!

Before going on to deal with the disposal of dead bodies, it may be advisable to write some more about the Tibetan views on death. Our attitude is quite different from that of Western peoples. To us a body is nothing more than a "shell", a material covering for the immortal spirit. To us a dead body is worth less than an old, worn-out suit of clothes. In the case of a person dying normally, that is, not by sudden unexpected violence, we consider the process to be like this: the body is diseased, faulty, and has become so uncomfortable for the spirit that no further lessons can be learned. So it is time to discard the body. Gradually the spirit withdraws and exteriorizes outside the flesh-body. The spirit form has exactly the same outline as the material version, and can very clearly be seen by a clairvoyant. At the moment of death, the cord joining the physical and spirit bodies (the "Silver Cord" of the Christian Bible) thins and parts, and the spirit drifts off. Death has then taken place. But birth into a new life, for the "cord" is similar to the umbilical cord which is severed to launch a new-born baby to a separate existence. At the moment of death the Glow of Life-force is extinguished from the head. This Glow also can be seen by a clairvoyant, and in the Christain Bible is referred to as "The Golden Bowl". Not being a Christian I am not familiar with the Book, but I believe there is a reference to "Lest the Silver Cord be severed, and the Golden Bowl be shattered".

Three days, we say, is the time it takes for a body to die, for all the physical activity to cease, and the spirit, soul, or ego, to become quite free of its fleshly envelope. We believe that there is an etheric double formed during the life of a body. This "double" can become a ghost. Probably everyone has looked at a strong light, and on turning away apparently saw the light still. We consider that life is electric, a field of force, and the etheric double remaining at death is similar to the light one sees *after* looking at a strong source, or, in electrical terms, it like a strong residual magnetic field. If the body had *strong* reasons for clinging to life, then there is a *strong* etheric which forms a ghost and haunts the familiar scenes. A miser may have such an attachment for his money-bags that he has his whole focus upon them. At death probably his last thought will be of fright concerning the fate of his money, so in his dying moment he adds to the strength of his etheric. The lucky recipient of the money-bags may feel somewhat uncomfortable in the small hours of the night. He may feel that "Old So-and-so is after his money again". Yes, he is right, Old So-and-so's ghost is probably very cross that his (spirit) hands cannot get a grip on that money!

There are three basic bodies; the flesh body in which the spirit can learn the hard lessons of life, the etheric, or "magnetic" body which is made by each of us by our lusts, greeds, and strong passions of various kinds. The third body is the spirit body, the "Immortal Soul". That is our Lamaist belief and not necessarily the orthodox Buddhist belief. A person dying has to go through three stages: his physical body has to be disposed of, his etheric has to be dissolved, and his spirit has to be helped on the road to the World of Spirit. The ancient Egyptians also believe in the etheric double, in the Guides of the Dead, and in the World of Spirit. In Tibet we helped people before they were dead. The adept had no need of such help, but the ordinary man or woman, or trappa, had to be guided the whole way through. It may be of interest to describe what happens.

One day the Honourable Master of Death sent for me. "It is time you studied the practical methods of Freeing the Soul, Lobsang. This day you shall accompany me."

We walked down long corridors, down slippery steps, and into the trappas' quarters. Here, in a "hospital room" an elderly monk was approaching that road we all must take. He had had a stroke and was very feeble. His strength was failing and his auric colours were fading as I watched. At all costs he had to be kept conscious until there was no more life to maintain that state. The lama with me took the old monk's hands and gently held them. "You are approaching the release from toils of the flesh, Old Man. Heed my words that you may choose the easy path. Your feet grow cold. Your life is edging up, closer and closer to its final escape. Compose your mind, Old Man, there is naught to fear. Life is leaving your legs, and your sight grows dim. The cold is creeping upwards, in the wake of your waning life. Compose your mind, Old Man, for there is naught to fear in the escape of life to the Greater Reality. The shadows of eternal night creep upon your sight, and your breath is rasping in your throat. The time draws near for the release of your throat. The time draws near for the release of your spirit to enjoy the pleasures of the After World. Compose yourself, Old Man. Your time of release is near."

The lama all the time was stroking the dying man from the collar bone to the top of his head in a way which has been proved to free the spirit painlessly. All the time he was being told of the pitfalls on the way, and how to avoid them. His route was exactly described, the route which has been mapped by those telepathic lamas who have passed over, and continued to talk by telepathy even from the next world.

"Your sight has gone, Old Man, and your breath is failing within you. Your body grows cold and the sounds of this life are no longer

174

heard by your ears. Compose yourself in peace, Old Man, for your death is now upon you. Follow the route we say, and peace and joy will be yours."

The stroking continued as the old man's aura began to diminish even more, and finally faded away. A sudden sharp explosive sound was uttered by the lama in an age-old ritual to completely free the struggling spirit. Above the still body the life-force gathered in a cloud-like mass, swirling and twisting as if in confusion, then forming into a smoke-like duplicate of the body to which it was still attached by the silver cord. Gradually the cord thinned, and as a baby is born when the umbilical cord is severed, so was the old man born into the next life. The cord thinned, became a mere wisp, and parted. Slowly, like a drifting cloud in the sky, or incense smoke in a temple, the form glided off. The lama continued giving instructions by telepathy to guide the spirit on the first stage of its journey. "You are dead. There is nothing more for you here. The ties of the flesh are severed. You are in Bardo. Go your way and we will go ours. Follow the route prescribed. Leave this, the World of Illusion, and enter into the Greater Reality. You are dead. Continue your way forward."

The clouds of incense rolled up, soothing the troubled air with its peaceful vibrations. In the distance drums were carrying out a rolling mutter. From some high point on the lamasery roof, a deep-toned trumpet sent its message crashing over the countryside. From the corridors outside came all the sounds of vigorous life, the "sussh sussh" of felt boots and, from somewhere, the grumbling roar of a yak. Here, in this little room, was silence. The silence of death. Only the telepathic instructions of the lama rippled the surface of the room's quiet. Death, another old man had gone on his long Round of Existences, profiting by his lessons in this life, maybe, but destined to continue until he reached Buddhahood by long, long effort.

We sat the body in the correct lotus posture and sent for those who prepare the bodies. Sent for others to continue the telepathic instruction of the departed spirit. For three days this continued, three days during which relays of lamas carried out their duties. On the morning of the fourth day one of the Ragyab came. He was from the Disposers of the Dead colony where the Lingkhor road branches to Dechhen Dzong. With his arrival, the lamas ceased their instruction, and the body was given over to the Disposer. He doubled it up into a tight circle and wrapped it in white cloth. With an easy swing, he lifted the bundle on to his shoulders and strode off. Outside he had a yak. Without hesitation he lashed the white mass on to the beast's back, and together they marched off. At the Place of the Breaking the Corpse Carrier would hand his burden to the Breakers of the Bodies. The "Place" was a desolate stretch of land dotted with huge boulders, and containing one large level stone slab, large enough to hold the biggest body. At the four corners of the slab there were holes in the stone, and posts driven in. Another stone slab had holes in it to half its depth.

The body would be placed upon the slab and the cloth stripped off. The arms and legs of the corpse would be tied to the four posts. Then the Head Breaker would take his long knife and slit open the body. Long gashes would be made so that the flesh could be peeled off in strips. Then the arms and legs would be sliced off and cut up. Finally, the head would be cut off and opened.

At first sight of the Corpse Carrier vultures would have come swooping out of the sky, to perch patiently on the rocks like a lot of spectators at an open-air theatre. These birds had a strict social order and any attempt by a presumptuous one to land before the leaders would result in a merciless mobbing.

By this time the Body Breaker would have the trunk of the corpse open. Plunging his hands into the cavity, he would bring out the heart, at sight of which the senior vulture would flap heavily to the ground and waddle forward to take the heart from the Breaker's outstretched hand. The next-in-order bird would flap down to take the liver and with it would retire to a rock to eat. Kidneys, intestines, would be divided and given to the "leader" birds. Then the strips of flesh would be cut up and given to the others. One bird would come back for half the brain and perhaps one eye, and another would come flapping down for yet another tasty morsel. In a surprisingly short time all the organs and flesh would have been eaten, leaving nothing but the bare bones remaining on the slab. The breakers would snap these into convenient sizes, like firewood, and would stuff them into the holes in the other slab. Heavy rammers would then be used to crush the bones to a fine powder. The birds would eat that!

These Body Breakers were highly skilled men. They took a pride in their work and for their own satisfaction they examined all the organs to determine the cause of death. Long experience had enabled them to do this with remarkable ease. There was, of course, no real reason why they should be so interested, but it was a matter of tradition to ascertain the illness causing "the spirit to depart from this vehicle." If a person had been poisoned—accidentally or deliberately—the fact soon became obvious. Certainly I found their skill of great benefit to me as I studied with them. I soon became very proficient at dissecting dead bodies. The Head

Breaker would stand beside me and point out features of interest: "This man, Honourable Lama, has died from a stoppage of blood to the heart. See, we will slit this artery, here, and—yes—here is a clot blocking the blood flow." Or it may be: "Now this woman, Honourable Lama, she has a peculiar look. A gland here must be at fault. We will cut it out and see." There would be a pause while he cut out a good lump, and then: "Here it is, we will open it; yes, it has a hard core inside."

So it would go on. The men were proud to show me all they could, they knew I was studying with them by direct order of the Inmost One. If I was not there, and a body looked as if it was particularly interesting, they would save it until I arrived. In this way I was able to examine hundreds of dead bodies, and definitely

I excelled at surgery later! This was far better training than the system whereby medical students have to share cadavers in hospital school dissecting-rooms. I know that I learned more anatomy with the Body Breakers than I did at a fully equipped medical school later.

In Tibet, bodies cannot be buried in the ground. The work would be too hard because of the rocky soil and the thinness of the earth covering. Nor is cremation possible on economic grounds; wood is scarce and to burn a body, timber would have to be imported from India and carried to Tibet across the mountains on the backs of yaks. The cost would be fantastic. Water disposal was not permissible either, for to cast dead bodies into the streams and rivers would pollute the drinking-water of the living. There is no other method open to us than air disposal, in which, as described, birds consume the flesh and the bones. It differs only from the Western method in two ways: Westerners bury bodies and let the worms take the place of birds. The second difference is that in the Western world the knowledge of the cause of death is buried with the body and no one knows if the death certificate really has stated the correct cause. Our Body Breakers *make sure* that they know what a person died of!

Everyone who dies in Tibet is "disposed of" in this way except the highest lamas, who are Previous Incarnations. These are embalmed and placed in a glass-fronted box where they can be seen in a temple, or embalmed and covered with gold. This latter process was most interesting. I took part in such preparations many times. Certain Americans who have read my notes on the subject cannot believe that we really used gold; they say that it would be beyond "even an American's skill"! Quite, we did not mass-produce things, but dealt with individual items as only the craftsman could. We in Tibet could not make a watch to sell for a dollar. But we *can* cover bodies in gold.

One evening I was called to the presence of the Abbot. He said: "A Previous Incarnation is shortly to leave his body. Now he is at the Rose Fence. I want you to be there so that you can observe the Preserving in Sacredness."

So once again I had to face the hardships of the saddle and journey to Sera. At that lamasery I was shown to the room of the old abbot. His auric colours were on the point of extinction, and about an hour later he passed from the body to the spirit. Being an abbot, and an erudite man, he had no need to be shown the path through the Bardo. Nor had we need to wait the usual three days. For that night only the body sat in the lotus attitude, while lamas kept their death watch.

In the morning, at the first light of day, we filed in solemn procession down through the main lamasery building: into the temple, and through a little-used door down to secret passages below. Ahead of me two lamas were carrying the body on a litter. It was still in the lotus position. From the monks behind came a deep chanting and, in the silences, the trill of a silver bell. We had on our red robes, and over them our yellow stoles. On the walls our shadows were thrown in flickering, dancing outline, exaggerated and distorted by the light of the butter-lamps and flaring torches. Down we went, down into secret places. At last, some fifty or sixty feet below the surface, we arrived at a sealed stone door. We entered: the room was ice-cold. The monks carefully set down the body, and then all departed except three lamas and I. Hundreds of butter-lamps were lit and provided a harsh yellow glare. Now the body was stripped of its vestments and carefully washed. Through the normal body orifices the internal organs were removed and placed into jars, which were carefully sealed. The inside of the body was thoroughly washed and dried, and a special form of lacquer was poured into it. This would form a hard crust inside the body, so that the outlines would be as in life. With the lacquer dry and hard, the body cavity was packed and padded with great care so as not to disturb the shape. More of the lacquer was poured in to saturate the padding and, in hardening, to provide a solid interior. The outer surface of the body was painted with lacquer and allowed to dry. Over the hardened surface a "peeling solution" was added, so that the thin sheets of filmy silk which were now to be pasted on, could later be removed without causing harm. At last the padding of silk was considered adequate. More lacquer (of a different type) was poured on, and the body was now ready for the next stage of the preparations. For a day and a night it was allowed to remain stationary so that final and complete drying could take place. At the end of that time we returned to the room to find the body quite hard and rigid and in the lotus position. We carried it in procession to another room beneath, which was a furnace so built that the flames and heat could circulate outside the walls of this room and so provide an even and high temperature.

The floor was thickly covered with a special powder, and in this, in the centre, we placed the body. Down below, monks were already preparing to light the fires. Carefully we packed the whole room tightly with a special salt from one district of Tibet, and a mixture of herbs and minerals. Then, with the room filled from floor to ceiling, we filed out of the corridor, and the door of the room was closed and sealed with the Seal of the Lamasery. The order to light the furnaces was given. Soon came the crackling of wood and the sizzling of burning butter as the flames spread. With the furnaces well alight, they would continue to burn yak-dung and waste butter. For a whole week the fire raged down below, sending clouds of hot air through the hollow walls of the Embalming Chamber. At the end of the seventh day no more fuel was added. Gradually the fires died down and flickered out. The heavy stone walls creaked and groaned in their cooling. Once more the corridor became cool enough to enter. For three days all was still as we all waited for the room to reach the normal temperature. On the eleventh day from the date of sealing, the Great Seal was broken and the door pushed open. Relays of monks scraped out the hardened compound with their hands. No tools were used in case the body was harmed. For two days the monks scraped away, crushing in the hands the friable salt compound. At last the room was empty—except for the shrouded body sitting so still in the centre, still in the lotus attitude. Carefully we lifted it and carried it to the other room where, in the light of the butter-lamps we would be able to see more clearly.

Now the silken coverings were peeled off one by one until the body alone remained. The preserving had been perfect. Except that it was much darker, the body might have been that of a sleeping man, who might at any time awaken. The contours were as in life and there was no shrinkage. Once again lacquer was applied to the naked dead body, and then the goldsmiths took over. These were men with a skill unsurpassed. Craftsmen. Men who could cover dead flesh with gold. Slowly they worked, layer upon layer of the thinnest, softest gold. Gold worth a fortune outside Tibet, but here valued only as a sacred metal—a metal that was incorruptible, and so symbolic of Man's final spirit state. The priest-goldsmiths worked with exquisite care, attentive to the minutest detail, so that when their work was finished they left as testimony of their skill a golden figure, exact as in life, with every line and wrinkle reproduced. Now the body, heavy with its gold, was carried to the Hall of Incarnations and, like the others there, set up on a gold throne. Here in this Hall there were figures dating back to the earliest times—sitting in rows, like solemn judges watching with half-closed eyes the frailties and failings of the present generation. We talked in whispers here and walked carefully, as if not to disturb the living-dead. To one body in particular I was attracted—some strange power held me fascinated before it. It seemed to gaze at me with an all-knowing smile. Just then there was a gentle touch on my arm, and I nearly dropped with fright. "That was *you*, Lobsang, in your last incarnation. We thought you would recognize it!"

My Guide led me to the next gold figure and remarked: "And that was I."

Silently, both much moved, we crept from the Hall and the door was sealed behind us.

Many times after I was allowed to enter that Hall and study the gold-clad figures. Sometimes I went alone and sat in meditation before them. Each has its written history, which I studied with the greatest interest. Here was the history of my present Guide, the Lama Mingyar Dondup, the story of what he had done in the past, a summary of his character and his abilities. The dignities and honours conferred upon him. The manner of his passing.

Here also was *my* past history and that, too, I studied with my full attention. Ninety-eight gold figures sat here in the Hall, in the hidden chamber carved from the rock, and with the well-concealed door. The history of Tibet was before me. Or so I thought. The earliest history was to be shown to me later.

CHAPTER SEVENTEEN

FINAL INITIATION

AFTER, at various lamaseries, I had seen the embalming some half-dozen times, I was one day sent for by the Abbot in charge of Chakpori. "My friend," said he, "on the direct order of the Precious One you are to be initiated as an abbot. As you have requested, you can—like Mingyar Dondup—continue to be addressed as 'lama'. I merely give the message of the Precious One."

So as a Recognized Incarnation, I had again the status with which I left the Earth some six hundred years before. The Wheel of Life had revolved full circle.

Some time later an aged lama came to my room and told me that now I must undergo the Ceremony of the Little Death. "For, my son, until you have passed the Gateway of Death, and returned, you cannot truly know that there *is* no death. Your studies in astral travelling have taken you far. This will take you much farther, beyond the realms of life, and into the past of our country."

The preparatory training was hard and prolonged. For three months I led a strictly supervised life. Special courses of horrible-tasting herbs added an unpleasant item to my daily menu. I was adjured to keep my thoughts "on that alone which is pure and holy". As if one had much choice in a lamasery! Even tsampa and tea had to be taken in less quantity. Rigid austerity, strict discipline, and long, long hours of meditation.

At last, after three months, the astrologers said that the time was now right, the portents were favourable. For twenty-four hours I fasted until I felt as empty as a temple drum. Then I was led down those hidden stairs and passages far below the Potala. Far down we went, flaring torches in the hands of the others, nothing in mine. Down through the corridors I had traversed before. At last we reached the end of the passage. Solid rock confronted us. But a whole boulder was swung aside at our

181

approach. Another path confronted us—a dark and narrow path, with the odour of stale air, spices, and incense. Several yards farther on we were stopped momentarily by a ponderous gold-sheathed door which was slowly opened to the accompaniment of protesting squeaks which echoed and re-echoed as if through a vast space. Here the torches were extinguished, and butter-lamps lit. We moved ahead into a hidden temple carved from the solid rock by volcanic action in days long past. These corridors and passages once had led molten lava to the mouth of a belching volcano. Now puny humans trod the way and thought that they were gods. But now, I thought, we must concentrate on the task at hand, and here was the Temple of Secret Wisdom.

Three abbots led me in. The rest of the lamaistic retinue had melted away in the darkness, as the dissolving memories of a dream. Three abbots, aged, desiccated with years and gladly awaiting their recall to the Heavenly Fields: three old men, perhaps the greatest metaphysicians in the whole of the world, ready to give me my final ordeal of initiation. Each carried in the right hand a butter-lamp, and in the left a thick stick of smouldering incense. Here the cold was intense, a strange cold seemingly not of this earth. The silence was profound: what faint sounds there were served merely to accentuate that silence. Our felt boots made no footfalls: we might have been ghosts gliding along. From the saffron brocade robes of the abbots there came a faint rustle. To my horror I felt tingles and shocks all over me. My hands glowed as if a fresh aura had been added. The abbots, I saw, were also glowing. The very, very dry air and the friction of our robes, had generated a static electric charge. An abbot passed me a short gold rod and whispered, "Hold this in your left hand and draw it along the wall as you walk and the discomfort will cease." I did, and with the first release of stored electricity nearly jumped out of my boots. After that it was painless.

One by one, butter-lamps flickered into life, lit by unseen hands. As the wavering yellow light increased, I saw gigantic figures, covered in gold, and some half-buried in uncut gems. A Buddha loomed out of the gloom, so huge that the light did not reach beyond the waist. Other forms were dimly seen; the images of devils, the representations of lust, and the forms of the trials which Man had to undergo before the realization of Self.

We approached a wall on which was painted a fifteen-foot Wheel of Life. In the flickering light it appeared to revolve and made the senses reel with it. On we went until I was sure we would crash into the rock. The leading abbot vanished: what I had imagined to be a dark shadow was a well-concealed door. This gave entrance to a path going down and down—a narrow, steep, winding path where the faint glow of the abbots' butter-lamps merely seemed to intensify the dark. We felt our way haltingly, stumbling, sometimes sliding. The air was heavy and oppressive and it felt as if the whole weight of the earth above was pressing down on us. I felt as if we were penetrating the heart of the world. A final bend in the tortuous passage, and a cavern opened to our view, a cavern of rock glittering with gold: veins of it—lumps of it. A layer of rock, a layer of gold, a layer of rock—so it went on. High, very high above us, gold glinted like stars in a dark night sky, as sharp specks of it caught and reflected back the faint light the lamps shed.

In the centre of the cavern was a shining black house—a house as if made of polished ebony. Strange symbols ran along its sides, and diagrams like those I had seen on the walls of the lake tunnel. We walked to the house and entered the wide, high door. Inside were three black stone coffins, curiously engraved and marked. There was no lid. I peered inside, and at the sight of the contents I caught my breath and felt suddenly faint.

"My son," exclaimed the leading abbot, "look upon these. They were gods in our land in the days before the mountains came. They walked our country when seas washed our shores, and when different stars were in the sky. Look, for none but Initiates have seen these."

I looked again, fascinated and awed. Three gold figures, nude, lay before us. Two male and one female. Every line, every mark was faithfully reproduced by the gold. But the size! The female was quite ten feet long as she lay, and the larger of the two males was not under fifteen feet. Their heads were large and somewhat conical at the top. The jaws were narrow, with a small, thin-lipped mouth. The nose was long and thin, while the eyes were straight and deeply recessed. No dead figures, these—they looked asleep. We moved quietly and spoke softly as if afraid they would awaken. I saw a coffin-lid to one side: on it was engraved a map of the heavens—but how very strange the stars appeared. My studies in astrology had made me quite familiar with the heavens at night: but this was very, very different.

The senior abbot turned to me and said: "You are about to become an Initiate, to see the Past and to know the Future. The strain will be very great. Many die of it, and many fail, but none leave here alive unless they pass. Are you prepared, and willing?"

I replied that I was. They led me to a stone slab lying between two coffins. Here at their instruction I sat in the lotus attitude,

183

with my legs folded, my spine erect, and the palms of my hands facing up.

Four sticks of incense were lighted, one for each coffin and one for my slab. The abbots each took a butter-lamp and filed out. With the heavy black door shut I was alone with the bodies of the age-old dead. Time passed as I meditated upon my stone slab. The butter-lamp which I had carried spluttered and went out. For a few moments its wick smouldered red and there was the odour of burning cloth, then even that faded and was gone.

I lay back on my slab and did the special breathing which I had been taught throughout the years. The silence and the dark were oppressive. Truly it was the silence of the grave.

Quite suddenly my body became rigid, cataleptic. My limbs became numb and icy cold. I had the sensation that I was dying, dying in that ancient tomb more than four hundred feet below the sunshine. A violent shuddering jerk within me, and the inaudible impression of a strange rustling and creaking as of old leather being unfolded. Gradually the tomb became suffused by a pale blue light, like moonlight on a high mountain-pass. I felt a swaying, a rising and falling. For a moment I could imagine that I was once more in a kite, tossing and jouncing at the end of the rope. Awareness dawned that I *was* floating above my flesh body. With awareness came movement. Like a puff of smoke I drifted as if on an unfelt wind. Above my head I saw a radiance, like a golden bowl. From my middle depended a cord of silver-blue. It pulsed with life and glowed with vitality.

I looked down at my supine body, now resting like a corpse amid corpses. Little differences between my body and those of the giant figures slowly became apparent. The study was absorbing. I thought of the petty conceit of present-day mankind and wondered how the materialists would explain the presence of these immense figures. I thought ... but then I became aware that *something* was disturbing my thoughts. I seemed that I was no longer alone. Snatches of conversation reached me, fragments of unspoken thoughts. Scattered pictures began to flash across my mental vision. From far away someone seemed to be tolling a great, deep-toned bell. Quickly it came nearer and nearer until at last it appeared to explode in my head, and I saw droplets of coloured light and flashes of unknown hues. My astral body was tossed and driven like a leaf upon a winter gale. Scurrying flecks of red-hot pain lashed across my consciousness. I felt alone, deserted, a waif in a tottering universe. Black fog descended upon me, and with it a calmness not of this world.

Slowly the utter blackness enfolding me rolled away. From

somewhere came the booming of the sea, and the hissing rattle of shingle under the drive of the waves. I could smell the salt-laden air, and the tang of the seaweed. This was a familiar scene: I lazily turned on my back, in the sun-warmed sand, and gazed up at the palm trees. But, part of me said, I had never seen the sea, never even *heard* of palm trees! From a nearby grove came the sound of laughing voices, voices that grew louder as a happy group of sun-bronzed people came into sight. Giants! All of them. I looked down, and saw that I, too, was a "giant". To my astral perceptions came the impressions: countless ages ago. Earth revolved nearer the sun, in the opposite direction. The days were shorter and warmer. Vast civilizations arose, and men knew more than they do now. From outer space came a wandering planet and struck the Earth a glancing blow. The Earth was sent reeling, out of its orbit, and turning in the opposite direction. Winds arose and battered the waters, which, under different gravitational pulls, heaped upon the land, and there were floods, universal floods. Earthquakes shook the world. Lands sank beneath the seas, and others arose. The warm and pleasant land which was Tibet ceased to be a seaside resort and shot some twelve thousand feet above the sea. Around the land mighty mountains appeared, belching out fuming lava. Far away in the highlands rifts were torn in the surface, and vegetation and fauna of a bygone age continued to flourish. But there is too much to write in a book, and some of my "astral initiation" is far too sacred and private to put into print.

Some time later I felt the visions fading and becoming dark. Gradually my consciousness, astral and physical, left me. Later I became uncomfortably aware that I was *cold*—cold with lying on a stone slab in the freezing darkness of a vault. Probing fingers of thought in my brain, "Yes, he has returned to us. We are coming!" Minutes passed, and a faint glow approached. Butter-lamps. The three old abbots.

"You have done well, my son. For three days you have lain here Now you have seen. Died. And lived."

Stiffly I climbed to my feet, swaying with weakness and hunger. Out from that never-to-be-forgotten chamber and up to the cold, cold air of the other passages. I was faint with hunger, and over-come with all that I had seen and experienced. I ate and drank my fill, and that night, as I lay down to sleep, I knew that soon I would have to leave Tibet, and go to the strange foreign countries, as foretold. But now I can say that they were and are stranger than I would have imagined possible!

CHAPTER EIGHTEEN

TIBET—FAREWELL!

A FEW days later, as my Guide and I were sitting beside the River of Happiness, a man came galloping by. Idly he gazed in our direction and recognized the Lama Mingyar Dondup. Instantly the dust at the horse's feet was aswirl with the violence of his stopping.

"I have a message from the Inmost One, for the Lama Lobsang Rampa."

From his pouch he pulled the long, familiar packet wrapped in the silk scarf of greeting. He handed it to me with a triple prostration, and backed away, mounted his horse, and galloped off.

Now I was much more assured; the events below the Potala had given me self-confidence. I opened the packet and read the message before passing it to my Guide—and friend—the Lama Mingyar Dondup.

"I have to go to the Inmost One at the Jewel Park in the morning. You have to go as well."

"One does not normally guess at the Precious Protector's remarks, Lobsang, but I feel that you will shortly be leaving for China, and I, well, as I told you, I shall soon be returning to the Heavenly Fields. Let us make the most of this day and of the scant time remaining."

In the morning I trod the familiar path to the Jewel Park, down the hill, across the road, and into the main gates. The Lama Mingyar Dondup walked with me. In both our minds was the thought that this was perhaps the last time we would make this

186

journey together. Perhaps it was reflected, too, strongly in my face, for when I saw the Dalai Lama alone, he said: "The time of parting, of taking fresh paths is always hard and fraught with misery. Here in this Pavilion I sat in meditation for hours, wondering if I would do right to stay or leave when our country was invaded. Either would cause pain to some. Your Path is straight ahead, Lobsang, and it is not an easy path for *anyone*. Family, friends, country—all must be left behind. The Path ahead contains, as you have been told, hardship, torture, misunderstanding, disbelief—all that is unpleasant. The ways of the foreigners are strange and not to be accounted for. As I told you once before, they believe only that which *they* can do, only that which can be tested in their Rooms of Science. Yet the greatest science of all, the Science of the Overself, they leave untouched. That is your Path, the Path you chose before you came to this Life. I have arranged for you to leave for China at the end of five days."

Five days! Five *days*! ! I have expected five weeks. As my Guide and I climbed up to our mountain home, no word was exchanged between us until we were again within the walls of the Temple.

"You will have to see your parents, Lobsang. I will send a messenger."

Parents? The Lama Mingyar Dondup had been more than a father and mother to me. And soon he would be leaving this life before I returned to Tibet in a few short years. All I would see of him then would be his gold-covered figure in the Hall of Incarnations—like an old, discarded robe for which the wearer had no further use.

Five days! Busy days. From the Potala Museum a new suit of Western clothes was brought for me to try on. Not that I was going to wear one in China, my lama robes would be more suitable there, but so that the others could see how I looked. Oh, that suit! Tight tubes of cloth that gripped my legs, so tight that I was afraid to bend. Now I knew why the Westerners could not sit in the lotus attitude: their clothes were too tight. Certainly I thought I was "ruined for life" by these tight tubes. They put a white shroud on me, and around my neck they tied a thick ribbon and pulled it tight as if they were going to strangle me. Over that they fitted a short piece of cloth with patches and holes behind, in which, they said, the Westerners kept things—instead of in a robe as we did. But the worst was yet to come. They put thick and heavy "gloves" on my feet and pulled them tight with black strings with metal ends. The beggars who went on hands and knees around the Lingkhor road sometimes used gloves similar to these on their hands, but they were wise enough to use good Tibetan felt boots on their feet. I felt that I would be crippled, and so would not be able to go to China. A black inverted bowl with an edge round it was put on my head, and I was told that I was dressed as a "Western gentleman of leisure". It seemed to me that they would *have* to have leisure, as surely they could not be expected to do any work dressed up like this!

On the third day I went again to my former home. Alone, on foot, as when I first set out. But this time as a lama, and as an abbot. Father and mother were at home to meet me. This time I was an honoured guest. In the evening of that day I again went to father's study, and signed my name and rank in the Family Book. Then I set off again, on foot, for the lamasery which had been my home for so long.

The remaining two days soon passed. On the evening of the last day I again saw the Dalai Lama and made my farewells and received his blessing. My heart was heavy as I took leave of him. The next time I would see him, as we both knew, would be when he was dead.

In the morning, at first light, we set out. Slowly, reluctantly. Once more I was homeless, going to strange places, and having to learn all over again. As we reached the high mountain-pass we turned to take a last long look at the Holy City of Lhasa. From the top of the Potala a solitary kite was flying.

"KINDNESS TO PUBLISHERS" DEPARTMENT

Throughout the years since "The Third Eye" first appeared I have had a tremendous amount of mail, and up to the present I have always answered that mail. Now I have to say that I am no longer able to reply to any mail at all unless adequate return postage is enclosed. So please do NOT send letters to my Publisher for forwarding to me because I have asked my Publisher not to forward any letters.

People forget that they pay for a BOOK, and NOT a lifetime of free post-paid advisory service. Publishers are PUBLISHERS—not a letter forwarding service.

I have had letters from all over the world, even from well behind the Iron Curtain, but not one in several thousand people encloses return postage, and the cost is so much that I can no longer undertake replies.

People ask such peculiar things, too. Here are just some:

There was a very desperate letter from Australia which reached me when I was in Ireland. The matter was (apparently) truly urgent, so at my own expense I sent a cable to Australia, and I did not even receive a note of thanks.

A certain gentleman in the U.S.A. wrote me a letter DEMANDING that I should immediately write a thesis for him and send it by return airmail. He wanted to use it as his thesis to obtain a Doctorate in Oriental Philosophy. Of course he did not enclose any postage; it was merely a somewhat threatening demand!

An Englishman wrote me a very, very haughty letter in the third person, demanding my credentials. And only if they were completely satisfactory to this person would he consider placing himself under my tuition, provided that there would be no charge for it. In other words, I was supposed to be honoured. (I do not think he would like my reply!)

Another one wrote to me and said that if I "and my chums" would come from Tibet and cluster around his bed in the astral at night then he would be able to feel more happy about astral travelling.

Other people write to me and ask me everything from high esoteric things (which I can answer if I want to) to how to keep hens and one's husband! People also consider that they should write to me just whenever they think they should, and then they get offensive if I do not reply by return airmail.

I will ask you NOT to bother my Publishers, in fact I have asked them not to send on any letters to me because they are in business as Publishers. For those who really do need an answer (although I do not invite letters) I have an accommodation address. It is:

> Dr T. Lobsang Rampa,
> BM/TLR,
> London W.C.1., England.

I do not guarantee any reply, and if you use this address you will have to provide very adequate postage because the letters will be forwarded to me and I shall have to pay, so I shall not be in a sweet enough mood to reply unless you have made my expense your expense. For example, it will cost me a dollar at least by the time forwarding charges are paid.

T. Lobsang Rampa

Rampa's Tranquilliser Touch-Stones

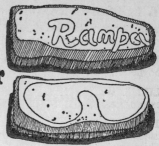

You are interested in the Higher Sciences or you would not be reading this book. Have you considered how your tranquillity can be nourished by a Rampa-Touch-Stone? On page 123 in *Wisdom of the Ancients* you can read about these Touch-Stones. They are available with simple instructions

AN INSTRUCTION RECORD ON MEDITATION

A large number of people wrote to Lobsang Rampa demanding a record about Meditation, so at last he has made the only special, fully authentic recording by him. Tells you how to meditate, shows you how easy it is, places peace, harmony and inner contentment within YOUR reach. A. Touch-Stones Ltd. can supply this 12" record AND THE TRANQUILLISER TOUCH STONE ANYWHERE at the prices below AIRMAIL FREE.

Price List	Record	Tranquilliser Touch-Stones	
Australia	5.50	4.20	dollars
Austria	90	120	schillings
Belgium	190	230	francs
Canada	7	5.50	dollars
Denmark	28	33.5	kroner
France	25	24	francs
Great Britain	1.80	1.85	pounds
Germany	14	18	deutsche marks
Holland	14.50	17	guilders
Italy	3440	2900	lires
New Zealand	5.50	4.20	dollars
Norway	25	32	kroner
S. Africa	6	3.80	rand
Sweden	24	25	kroner
U.S.A.	7	5	dollars
All other places	2.80	1.90	£
All other places	7	5	dollars

A. TOUCH-STONES LTD. Dept. A.
33 Ashby Road
Loughborough
Leicestershire LE11 3AA
England

is the author of fourteen extraordinary books, each one immensely readable and thought provoking:

THE SAFFRON ROBE: The personal story of Lobsang Rampa's boyhood at the great Lamasery of Potala.   35p

LIVING WITH THE LAMA: More details of Lobsang Rampa's extraordinary existence – this time from a different angle!   35p

THE THIRD EYE: A great bestseller wherever it has been published. This tells how Lobsang Rampa was given the power of the Third Eye.   50p

DOCTOR FROM LHASA: In which Lobsang Rampa proved that mortal man can discipline his mind and body to survive starvation and torture.   40p

THE RAMPA STORY: Revealing other aspects of the author's strange life and the mystic powers with which he is endowed.   40p

WISDOM OF THE ANCIENTS: A book of knowledge with special sections on breathing exercises and diet.   50p

YOU – FOREVER: A special course of instruction in psychic development and metaphysics.   35p

THE CAVE OF THE ANCIENTS: Lobsang Rampa's story of his experiences at the Lamaseries of Tibet.   50p

CHAPTERS OF LIFE: Predictions and comments on the events taking place in the astral world.   Illustrated 40p

BEYOND THE TENTH: Lobsang Rampa explores the spiritual potential inherent in every human being.   35p

FEEDING THE FLAME: In his first ten books Lobsang Rampa has tried to light a candle, or possibly two. In this, the eleventh book, he is trying to feed the flame.   50p

THE HERMIT: A young monk receives the wisdom of the ages from an old, blind hermit.   35p

THE THIRTEENTH CANDLE: Lobsang Rampa answers questions about the world of the astral, healing, life after death and many more.   35p

CANDLELIGHT: More questions answered about aspects of metaphysics – pendulums, dowsing, levitation and teleportation, etc.   40p

ALL AVAILABLE IN CORGI BOOKS

A SELECTED LIST OF PSYCHIC, MYSTIC AND OCCULT BOOKS THAT APPEAR IN CORGI

All these books are available at your bookshop or newsagent: or can be ordered direct from the publisher. Just tick the titles you want and fill in the form below.

CORGI BOOKS, Cash Sales Department, P.O. Box 11, Falmouth, Cornwall.

Please send cheque or postal order, no currency.

U.K. and Eire: send 15p for first book plus 5p per copy for each additional book ordered to a maximum charge of 50p to cover the cost of postage and packing.

Overseas Customers and B.F.P.O.: allow 20p for first book and 10p per copy for each additional book.

NAME ....

ADDRESS ....

(JULY, 75) ....

While every effort is made to keep prices low, it is sometimes necessary to increase prices at short notice. Corgi Books reserve the right to show new retail prices on covers which may differ from those previously advertised in the text or elsewhere.